Law for Social Workers:
An Introduction

Second Edition

Law for Social Workers: An Introduction

Second Edition

Caroline Ball

ASHGATE

First published by Wildwood House Limited.

This edition published by
Ashgate
Ashgate Publishing Limited
Gower House
Croft Road
Aldershot
Hants GU11 3HR
England

Ashgate Publishing Company
Old Post Road
Brookfield
Vermont 05036
USA

A CIP catalogue record for this book is available from the British Library and the US Library of Congress

ISBN 1 85742 067 5

Typeset in 11pt Times by Poole Typesetting (Wessex) Ltd, Bournemouth and printed in Great Britain by Billing & Sons Ltd, Worcester.

Contents

PART III THE LEGAL CONTEXT OF WORK WITH OTHER CLIENT GROUPS

Table of cases

Abbreviations for law reports

A.C.   Law Reports: Appeal Cases
All E.R. All England Law Reports
Fam.   Law Reports: Family
F.L.R.   Family Law Reports
W.L.R.   Weekly Law Reports

Table of statutes

Adoption of Children Act 1926 (repealed)
Adoption Act 1976
Bail Act 1976
Child Abduction Act 1984
Children Act 1989
Children and Young Persons Act 1933
Children and Young Persons Act 1969
Chronically Sick and Disabled Persons Act 1970
Courts and Legal Services Act 1990
Criminal Justice Act 1982
Criminal Justice Act 1988
Criminal Justice Act 1991
Criminal Law Act 1977
Disabled Persons (Services, Consultation and Representation) Act 1986
Domestic Proceedings and Magistrates' Courts Act 1978
Domestic Violence and Matrimonial Proceedings Act 1976
Education Act 1944
Education Act 1980
Education Act 1981
Housing (Homeless Persons) Act 1977 (repealed)
Housing Act 1985
Matrimonial Causes Act 1973
Matrimonial Homes Act 1983
Mental Health Act 1959
Mental Health (Amendment) Act 1982 (repealed)

Mental Health Act 1983
National Assistance Act 1948
National Assistance (Amendment) Act 1951
National Health Service and Community Care Act 1990
Police and Criminal Evidence Act 1984
Protection from Eviction Act 1977
Social Security Act 1986
Supreme Court Act 1981

Statutory instruments
Adoption Agency Regulations 1983 (No. 1964)
Adoption Rules 1984 (No. 265)
Adoption (Amendment) Rules 1991
Children (Admissibility of Hearsay Evidence) Order 1991
Family Proceedings Rules 1991
Family Proceedings Court (Children Act) Rules 1991
Magistrates' Courts (Advance Information) Rules 1985 (No. 601)
Mental Health (Hospital Guardianship and Consent to Treatment) Regulations 1983 (No. 893)
Secure Accommodation Regulations 1991
Secure Accommodation (No. 2) Regulations 1991

Acknowledgements

This book owes much to the experience of teaching law to students on the MA in Social Work course at the University of East Anglia (UEA), and to discussion, and occasionally fierce debate, with colleagues similarly engaged at other institutions, as well as legal and social work practitioners. The content has also been informed by regular contact with guardians ad litem in the East Anglian region, and training involvement with the probation service and local authority social services departments.

It is a reflection of the speed of change in major areas of law affecting social work practice that a new edition, requiring very substantial re-writing, has had to be produced within three years of publication of the first edition. The law is as it stood on 1 December 1991 apart from the fact that the Criminal Justice Act 1991, due for implementation in the Autumn of 1992, is referred to as though already in force.

I am once again grateful for the opportunity to record publicly my gratitude to colleagues in the School of Social Work at UEA who are a constant source of stimulation and support, and especially to Martin Davies for his creative encouragement over many years, and June Thoburn for her child care expertise and the pleasures of joint teaching in that area. Having said that all errors and omissions are entirely my own.

PART I
THE LEGAL CONTEXT OF SOCIAL WORK PRACTICE

1 Nature, sources and administration of law

The law, by which is meant the body of rules whereby a civilized society maintains order and regulates its internal affairs as between one individual and another, and between individuals and the state, consists in the UK of common law, statute law (Acts of Parliament) and case law, or judicial precedent. For historical reasons the law of England and Wales profoundly differs from that of Scotland, and in important respects, particularly as regards children and young persons, from that of Northern Ireland; any reference to particular provisions therefore relate only to England and Wales unless the contrary is stated.

Parliament can, subject, in any conflict to the supremacy of European Economic Community Law, by statute, make or change the law in any way that a majority decision of both the House of Commons and the House of Lords, following established procedure, deems appropriate. The judges of the superior courts through their interpretation of statutory provisions and legal principles both define and refine existing law, and may, on occasions, where there is no similar case or established legal principle to which they can refer, make new law. Where judges do 'make' law in this way, Parliament may, by statute, subsequently restate the law to its own liking. The process of legislation from political or practical ideas through the democratic process to enacted statute is a familiar one, the interpreting and occasional making of law by the judges may be less so.

In order to understand the working of judicial precedent it is necessary to look at the structure of the courts and the way in which decisions in the superior courts have to be followed by those below them in the hierarchy (Figures 1 and 2). The courts within which the law is administered reflect the essential difference between the civil and criminal law. Civil law, for the most part, involves disputes between individual parties, with one seeking either an order, or compensation for loss or damage suffered, against another. The criminal law is concerned with the trial and punishment of those who have acted in a way that is unlawful; this includes, of course, besides acts generally recognized as crimes such as murder, rape and theft, a vast range of matters, such as minor motoring offences, which are only technically 'criminal' in nature but none the less come within the jurisdiction of the criminal courts.

As can be seen from the figures, the separate systems of courts for the administration of the criminal and civil law now come together only when an appeal reaches the House of Lords, or more rarely the European Court.

Judicial precedent – the system by which the decisions of superior courts are binding on those below them in the hierarchy – not only clarifies and refines the law, but makes it more certain. Where a point of law has been decided in a previous case, a court subsequently hearing a case involving the same point will be bound to follow that decision or differentiate the circumstances of the current case.

A point of law decided in a case in the House of Lords is binding on all other courts below – but not necessarily on itself on a future occasion (Practice Statement (Judicial Precedent) 1966). Decisions in either division of the Court of Appeal bind all the courts below and will generally be followed in their own subsequent decisions. In the High Court, divisional court decisions are binding on judges sitting alone, but one High Court judge's decision will not necessarily be binding – although it is likely to be influential – on another.

The inferior courts, which are the county court, lower tier of the Crown Court and all the magistrates' courts are bound by the decisions of all superior courts, but not by their own or those of other inferior courts.

Information on all important judicial decisions is recorded in reports in which the facts of the case, the points of law involved and the decision are recorded and published accord-

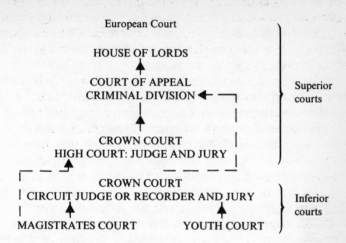

Figure 1   The criminal courts

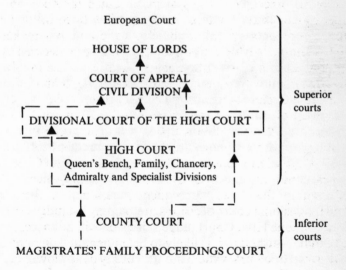

Figure 2   The civil courts

Key
Appeals — —▶ —

ing to the specialist subject-matter involved. There is an elaborate system of referencing to enable lawers and courts to keep track of developments in case law and to trace decisions relevant to particular situations or legal principles (see Glossary).

Jurisdiction of the courts
The civil courts

The venue for civil trials will depend either on the nature of the dispute or the sum of money involved, or sometimes both. As an example, it may be helpful to look first at family proceedings and then at other civil disputes.

One of the complicating factors about child care and family law is that in many proceedings, though not in divorce which cannot be heard by the magistrates, the family proceedings court, the county court and the High Court have concurrent jurisdiction. It may be a matter of chance, or more probably of a solicitor's preference, whether proceedings such as adoption or an application for a residence order, for instance, are heard in the family proceedings court or the county court, although as a matter of principle legal aid is only available for the least expensive proceedings which will provide the required order or remedy. Again, mainly on account of the cost, only the most complex cases go to the Family Division of the High Court. We look, in greater detail, at family and matrimonial proceedings, in outline, in Chapter 5, and child care and protection in Chapters 6–8.

Cases such as those involving claims for personal injury or breach of contract will generally be heard in the county court and in the Queen's Bench Division of the High Court only if very large sums of money are involved. Almost all these cases are eventually settled between the parties before the case actually reaches the court, or when it is part-heard.

Appeals from the magistrates' family proceedings go to the Family Division of the High Court and from the county and High Courts to the Court of Appeal Civil Division. From there they may, with leave, go to the House of Lords and the European Court.

Criminal courts

All criminal cases concerning adults (aged 18 years and over) start in the magistrates' court and most are dealt with there.

More serious cases, or those in which the defendant has a right to, and elects, trial by jury will be committed to the Crown Court for trial. Except in inner London and other metropolitan areas where paid and legally qualified stipendiary magistrates sit alone, the magistrates' courts are staffed by unpaid lay justices, appointed by a process which has in the past often seemed somewhat secretive. In order to overcome this in 1988 the Lord Chancellor ordered that from 1992 onwards the names of members of local Advisory Committees on the appointment of magistrates should be made public.

In the magistrates' court the justices, usually a chairman and two others, sit with a clerk whose role is to administer the court and advise on the law and other related legal issues such as evidence and procedure. The justices are responsible for all decisions whether they relate to the facts, the law or sentence, and these can be appealed against to the Crown Court, or on a point of law only to the Divisional Court.

About 95 per cent of all criminal cases begin and end with the magistrates; however, in more serious cases the justices will have to decide whether to commit to the Crown Court on bail or to remand the defendant in custody to await trial. Cases committed to the Crown Court will generally be heard in the second tier by a circuit judge or a recorder, possibly sitting with two lay justices and, if the defendant is pleading not guilty, a jury of twelve laymen whose role is to determine guilt or innocence. Murder and some other very serious or complex cases will be heard in the top tier of the Crown Court by a High Court judge, again sitting with a jury if the offence is denied.

Appeals against findings of guilt, or against sentences imposed by the magistrates, are heard in the Crown Court. Those from the Crown Court, against sentence or on a point of law, but not generally against the jury's finding of guilt unless that can be seen to be perverse in view of the judge's summing up of the evidence, are heard by the Criminal Division of the Court of Appeal. On a point of law only, and with the leave of the court, there may be a further appeal to the House of Lords and possibly afterwards to the European Court. (The criminal jurisdiction of the youth court is considered in Chapter 11.)

Access to legal advice and representation
The legal profession is currently divided into two fairly rigidly separated branches. Various attempts have been made to fuse aspects of their work but currently solicitors have a monopoly of direct access to clients and as a general rule only barristers have a right to be heard in the superior courts. Although some solicitors specialize in representing their clients in the courts to which they have access, most of their work is outside the courts, and most barristers do mainly advocacy work.

In order to help the public, most of whom will have occasion to seek professional legal advice only rarely, in their choice of a solicitor suitable to their needs the Law Society publishes lists of firms and legal advice centres, indicating their areas of expertise and whether they undertake legal aid work. Importantly, they have also established a child care panel whose members have specialist knowledge and experience and should be chosen for care and related proceedings in which good representation is essential for all parties.

Legal aid
The legal aid scheme was designed to ensure that access to the law, by way of advice and where necessary representation, is available to those unable to afford to pay for it themselves. Basically there are four types of legal aid in addition to the free duty solicitor scheme which operates in the criminal courts: legal advice and basic assistance under the 'green form' scheme, assistance by way of representation, criminal legal aid and civil legal aid. They depend on separate financial conditions, though the same basic principles apply, namely that the granting of legal aid is dependent on the reasonableness of the client's claim for the service and on his/her means, in terms of disposable income and capital, on which liability to pay, at all, in part, or in full, will be assessed (Burrows, 1989). Current administration of the scheme and government attempts to curtail spending effectively limit entitlement to legal aid to those on very low incomes.

Under the so-called 'green form' scheme, those who qualify financially are entitled to a variety of advice and basic help from a solicitor up to a cost of (currently) £50 or £90 for a petitioner for an undefended divorce or judicial separation. Assistance by way of representative covers the cost of a solicitor preparing a case and representing a party in most proceedings in magistrates' family proceedings courts. It is also available to patients appearing before Mental Health Review Tribunals.

Legal aid for criminal proceedings is granted by the clerk to the justices in the magistrates' court on the basis of the defendant's means and the desirability of his/her being legally represented in the interests of justice, as defined by the criteria laid down by a committee chaired by Lord Widgery (HMSO, 1966). If the clerk to whom application is made considers refusing legal aid, he must put the matter to a magistrate for a decision, subject to the general rule that doubts should be resolved in the defendant's favour. Annually published statistics show an enormous discrepancy between the refusal rates of different courts.

Legal aid for civil proceedings will cover all work leading up to and including representation in court proceedings, by a barrister if necessary. Civil legal aid is not available for cases covered by assistance by way of representation, or for the coroner's court, or most tribunals, though it is available for those appearing before employment appeal tribunals. The success of an application, which must be made by a solicitor to the legal aid office local committee, will depend on the applicant's financial eligibility, as assessed by the DSS, and the committee's view of the reasonableness of the case. Even if eligible for legal aid, litigants may be required to make substantial contributions towards the cost of their representation and, if successful, will have to reimburse the fund.

Support for unrepresented clients

Any litigant in criminal or civil proceedings who is not legally represented may have the assistance of someone, whether legally qualified or not, to sit beside him/her in court, taking notes, offering advice and suggesting questions to be asked. This may be an important role for a social worker to play for an inarticulate client who has been refused legal aid. This adviser, formerly called a 'McKenzie friend', may not address the court but may offer all other advice and assistance provided that the assistance is bona fide and not proferred in a way that is 'inimicable to the proper administration of justice' per Donaldson MR in *R.* v. *Leicester City Council ex parte Barrow and Another* [1991], see also *McKenzie* v. *McKenzie* [1970].

Standard of proof and rules of evidence

Since possibly liberty, and certainly reputation, may be at stake, a higher standard of proof is required for a conviction in criminal proceedings than for that in civil proceedings. Fashions change and, in criminal cases, there was for a few years a swing away from the generally accepted formula that the court should be 'satisfied beyond reasonable doubt' of the defendant's guilt to the court being 'sure' of it. More recently, 'reasonable doubt' appears to have found favour again. However phrased, it is clearly a higher standard than that in civil proceedings, where the issue is one between theoretically equal parties and the court is therefore required to base its decision only on a balance of probabilities in favour of one side or the other.

The law of evidence is for the most part detailed, highly complex and inextricably interwoven with the procedural rules for different proceedings – and best left to lawyers. However, as social workers are often called on to give evidence in court, the basic principles and the extent to which the effective presentation of relevant facts often determines the outcome of care and related proceedings make it essential that social workers have some understanding of the nature of evidence, and of two of the basic rules – those against hearsay evidence and the asking of leading questions.

Evidence in court consists of the testimony of witnesses given under oath and subject to cross-examination and, subject to many procedural safeguards, the contents of some documents and video recordings. The rules which exclude certain testimony and documents generally hinge on the principle that evidence must be the best available and must be reliable.

Hearsay, that is the evidence of a statement made by a person who is not giving evidence, in the attempt to establish the truth of what was said, is generally excluded both on grounds of not being the best available and not being reliable, in that it is not subject to cross-examination. If the truth of that statement is to be established, then the person who made it must be called to give evidence as to what they said. There are many practical exceptions to the rule against hearsay – e.g. it has to be relaxed in regard to social inquiry and similar reports. The rule against hearsay has also been relaxed in relation to evidence given in family proceedings in connection with the 'upbringing, maintenance or welfare of a child' (*The Children (Admissibility of Hearsay Evidence) Order* 1991).

Leading questions are not, contrary to popular belief, ones the answers to which might prove embarrassing or incriminating, but those which suggest the answer required. In order that witnesses give their own evidence and are not led into making the statements that their advocate might want them to make, leading questions may only be asked of witnesses giving their own testimony when the facts are not in dispute. They may be used in cross-examination because the nature of this is to test the accuracy of evidence already given under oath.

Tribunals

There are several administrative tribunals, such as Mental Health Review Tribunals and Social Security Appeals Tribunals, which exercise a quasi-judicial function outside the court system. Mainly these tribunals exist to determine appeals from administrative decisions and are mostly staffed by experts in the particular field, or by lay people representing the community, generally with a legally qualified chairperson. Proceedings are less formal than in courts and legal aid is not normally available for representation. This is therefore an area in which social workers and volunteers can play an important advocacy role. Although they are not courts of law, tribunals may possess case law of their own which they follow and they are, in any event, bound by the rules of natural justice (see below).

The Ombudsman

The terms of reference of the Ombudsman – properly the Parliamentary Commissioner for Administration – are to investigate complaints by individuals or corporate bodies who claim to have sustained injustice in consequence of maladministration. In practice, individuals can only approach the Ombudsman through their Member of Parliament. The Ombudsman possesses wide investigatory powers and, although he cannot alter or rescind decisions, as a result of his investigations departments very often take such action or make *ex gratia* payment of compensation.

Complaints about the National Health Service are investigated by the Health Service Commissioner, and against maladministration by local authorities by three Local Commissioners for Administration (Street and Brazier, 1986).

Representation and complaints procedures

Under the National Health Service and Community Care Act 1990 and the Children Act 1989 all local authorities are required to set up a procedure for considering representations, including complaints, which are made to them by a 'qualifying' individual, or anyone acting on their behalf. This definition covers any person whose need has come to the attention of the authority, and for whom the authority has a power or duty to provide or secure provision of a social service.

The local authority has to appoint a coordinating officer and publicize the complaints procedure. When a representation is made and the matter cannot be settled informally the complainant will be invited to make written representations to which the authority must respond. If the matter cannot be settled those representations will be heard by a panel established for the purpose with a chairman who is independent of the Authority. The panel makes recommendations to the Director of Social Services.

Natural justice

The rules of natural justice provide minimal standards for fair decision-making; these apply not only in courts and tribunals, but also to any public bodies who are under a duty to act judicially. This duty to act fairly in a judicial role is founded on two principles: the rule against bias, for instance, direct financial proprietary interest in the outcome of proceedings or knowledge of one of the litigants which might distort judgement, and the right to a fair hearing, encapsulated in the Latin tag, *audi alterem partem* ('hear both sides equally'). If a breach of natural justice can be established, the injured party is granted leave to seek redress, through judicial review by the High Court, of the proceedings in which the unfair treatment is alleged to have occurred.

The case of *R.* v. *West Malling Juvenile Court, ex parte K.* [1986] provides an example of a remedy for a breach of natural justice.

> Care proceedings under the Children and Young Persons Act 1969 were initiated by the local authority in respect of three children who had been looked after by their father, with considerable social work help, for three years after the death of his wife. Separate representation was ordered and a guardian ad litem (GAL) appointed. The father's solicitor

tried unsuccessfully to obtain details of any allegations made against the father before the hearing. On the morning of the hearing copies of the welfare and GAL's reports, which made serious allegations concerning the father's care of the children, were served on his advisers. They wished for time to prepare their case and call further evidence to rebut the allegations. The magistrates refused application for an adjournment and proceeded with the hearing. Care orders were made in respect of each child. The father successfully appealed by way of judicial review to quash the care orders on the grounds that he had good reason to feel that he had not had a fair hearing because the justices had refused an adjournment to allow him to prepare a response to the allegations made in the reports.

2 Housing, education, welfare rights and discrimination

This chapter brings together four areas of the client's life, housing, education, welfare rights and discrimination, in which social workers may be called on to recognize the legal nature of a problem or be helped to give appropriate advice or practical assistance in support of a client's rights by their understanding of the legal framework. For more detailed information a reference book such as *The Legal Rights Manual* (Cooper, 1990), is recommended.

Housing

Modern housing law is about the right of an occupier not to be unreasonably deprived of his/her home and only to pay a fair rent for it, the efforts of landlords to let out their property at the greatest profit and yet retain the greatest freedom of disposal of it, and the rule of law through the courts which determines the rights and wrongs of a particular situation and interprets the application of statute law to particular arrangements.

Housing law is a vast and complex subject best left to lawyers; however, there are three topics about which social workers need sufficient knowledge to advise their clients:

1. Eviction.
2. Unlawful eviction and harassment.
3. Homeless persons (Housing Act 1985, Part III).

These topics need to be looked at in some detail, after a short introduction on the different possible relationship that may exist between individuals and the 'land' (including any building on that land) that they occupy:

1. They may *own* the land – as freehold owner; or
2. They may have been granted exclusive use of the land for a slice of time in return for payment or services as tenant; or
3. They may have permission to be on the land as the licensee without having a tenancy (as are guests in hotels, residents in hospitals or homes, children in their parents' homes, etc.); or
4. They may be on the land without permission as a trespasser.

The occuper's rights and duties are determined by his/her relationship to the land. In particular, the distinction between a *tenant* and a *licensee* is important because tenants have much statutory protection from eviction and rent increases under the Rent and Housing Acts and licensees have very little, although they may be entitled to protection from immediate eviction. Trespassers have no protection, except for recourse to the courts if undue force is used against them.

It is an overriding principle that it is the law, and not the parties, which determines the form of the relationship. A landlord may not, for instance, evade the consequences of what is effectively a tenancy by describing the tenant as a 'licensee'.

Eviction
If a landlord wishes to regain possession of his property, he can only do so, whether or not the tenancy is at an end, if the tenant agrees (without unlawful pressure, see p. 16) to leave. If the tenant does not agree to leave, and

(a) the tenant breaks a term of the lease or tenancy agreement;
(b) the tenant is paying on a weekly or monthly basis and protected by the Rent Acts;
(c) the tenant is paying on a weekly or monthly basis but is not protected by the Rent Acts

then the landlord must give valid notice to quit and get an

eviction order from the county court. Only then will he be entitled to evict the tenant, with the help of the bailiff if necessary.

It is important for social workers to advise their clients that they should not leave on threat of a court order, and that unless they are agreeable to leaving, any tenant served with a county court summons for possession should seek immediate legal advice (currently available under the 'greenform' scheme) as to their rights and how to contest the landlord's application. Although they may not be ultimately successful in retaining the accommodation, they may well be able to get an extension of time before the eviction order can be executed. If no application is made to the court on behalf of the tenant, the landlord may, provided the formalities are satisfied, be granted an immediate eviction order.

Unlawful eviction and harassment

People are unlawfully evicted if they are physically evicted from premises they are entitled (see above) to occupy without an eviction order being in force. Harassment consists of making life so unpleasant that the tenant leaves, or stays but fails to complain to the rent officer or public health inspector of the treatment he/she is subjected to. Both unlawful eviction and harassment are actionable as criminal proceedings under the Protection from Eviction Act 1977 as amended by the Housing Act 1988, or civil proceedings. In civil proceedings damages may be very substantial as they can be awarded to reflect the difference between the value to the landlord of the tenant's property or vacant possession.

The 'Residential Occupier' referred to in the definitions in section 1(2) and 1(3) of the 1977 Act protects almost anyone living on premises, except certain trespassers or licensees whose licence has ended.

All in all, landlords are well advised always to seek a court order before evicting an occupier, and social workers should act at once to seek legal advice on behalf of a client threatened with eviction who is more likely to be protected as a 'residential occupier' than not (Cooper, 1990).

Criminal proceedings are only rarely brought, usually by the Tenancy Relations or Harassment Officer of the local authority. Where they are brought, the delay is often too great to benefit the evicted person except, possibly, in terms of compensation. Civil proceedings may be brought in the county court (or High Court if large damages are sought). The injured party may seek an injunction, an order of the court which identifies the person bound by it and makes him liable if he fails to comply with it for contempt of court which can be dealt with by fine or imprisonment.

A full injunction is normally made at the end of lengthy proceedings but in an emergency an occupier who can be shown to have acted without delay may apply with an affidavit to a court or a judge in chambers for an *ex parte* injunction which will last for a few days until a court hearing *inter partes*. At the *inter partes* hearing the court may issue an interim injunction to last until the full hearing.

At the full hearing damages may be awarded. They may be special – to cover actual loss; or general – for shock and injury; or aggravated – when the treatment was particularly brutal or offensive; or exemplary – to teach the landlord a lesson.

In order to help a client to obtain relief, speed and specialist legal advice from a Law Centre or a private practitioner is essential. It is important to make note of any incidents which may amount to harassment for use as evidence.

Homeless persons

The basic aims of the Housing (Homeless Persons) Act 1977, the provisions of which are now consolidated into the Housing Act 1985, Part III, were to impose on local housing authorities a statutory duty to rehouse homeless families, and to provide clear guidelines for determining whether a homeless family falls within the responsibility of one local authority rather than another. The policy of the Act is to keep families together by placing on local housing authorities a duty to provide full and permanent rehousing for those who satisfy the qualifying conditions. A substantial body of case law has grown up around the statutory provisions. In order to qualify for full and permanent rehousing certain criteria have to be satisfied, as follows.

Homelessness which is not intentional   The applicant must be homeless and must not be intentionally so. Section 58 of the Housing Act 1985 defines a person as being 'homeless' if he has no accommodation available for occupation by himself together with any member of his family living with him and any other person who normally lives with him 'in circumstances which the housing authority considers it reasonable for that person to do so'. Accommodation is 'available' if there is some place which the claimant is entitled to occupy as owner or tenant, or he has a court order entitling him to occupy. In the same way, an occupier who has a contractual or bare licence or entitlement to occupy because the landlord has not obtained a possession order, and eviction would be unlawful, cannot qualify as homeless under the Act. On the other hand, lack of a place to park a mobile home or moor a houseboat counts as 'homelessness'.

If the authority seeks to avoid responsibility for rehousing on the ground that the applicant is intentionally homeless, the onus of proof is on them. Under section 60 of the 1985 Act, it is stated:

> A person becomes homeless intentionally if he deliberately does or fails to do anything in consequence of which he ceases to occupy accommodation which is available for his occupation and which it would have been reasonable for him to occupy [e.g. fails to pay the rent and is lawfully evicted].

However, if the loss of accommodation arises from genuine ignorance of a legal right to continue occupation, the person should not be treated as being intentionally homeless. This might occur where a tenant, given notice to quit, left premises because he/she was unaware of the right to remain in occupation until the expiry of a court order.

Priority need   The original legislation was designed to protect vulnerable people and to ensure that lack of a home would not result in families being split up. Prior to the 1977 Act, homeless families were often in a catch-22 situation where the children were in care because of lack of accommodation and the parents were not entitled to accommodation because the children were in care. Under the 1985 Act, a person has priority need if:

(a)   he has dependent children living with him, or who might reasonably be expected to live with him;

(b)   he becomes homeless through flood, fire or other disaster;

(c)   he or anyone who lives or might reasonably be expected to live with him is especially vulnerable because of age, disability or other special reasons;

(d)   she, or a woman who does or might reasonably be expected to live with the applicant, is pregnant.

Those who have a priority need but may have become intentionally homeless are entitled to temporary accommodation (e.g. bed and breakfast) to give them a chance to make permanent arrangements, and homeless people without a priority need may receive a lesser degree of assistance.

A local connection   Applicants must be accepted by the authority to which they apply 'unless he and anyone who might reasonably be expected to live with him has no connection with that authority and does have a connection with another' (1985 Act, s.61). A person may have a local connection because he either lives, or once lived, in an area, or because he is employed there, or because of family connections, or any special circumstances. Anyone who is homeless as a result of domestic violence does not have to establish a local connection in the area to which he/she applies.

It will be apparent that given the amount of case law that has built up around the provisions specialist legal advice may be essential in complex cases.

In a situation in which there are more homeless people than available housing, many authorities are under intolerable strain. Until 1986 dissatisfied claimants frequently, and often successfully, resorted to judicial review since it provided the only effective appeal against a housing authority's decision in cases under the Act. The decision of the House of Lords in *Puhlhofer* v. *London Borough of Hillingdon* [1986], that judicial review should not be regarded as the normal remedy for the lack of any other right of appeal but should only be available in exceptional cases, has substantially reduced the number of applications.

Education

Local authorities have considerable statutory obligations under the Education Act 1944, as amended by subsequent Education Acts, to provide and maintain an efficient education service and to ensure that parents, guardians and others caring for children meet their obligations in respect of the children's education; the legislation in this field is both detailed and, because of its vulnerability to political whim, prone to frequent change. In terms of their practice, it is suggested that there are two areas of education law with which social workers need to be familiar: the legal consequences following from parental failure to ensure a child's attendance at school, and the statutory provisions regarding children with special educational needs.

School attendance

The legal duty to ensure attendance rests with parents or guardians or, in practice, anyone else caring for a child *in loco parentes*. Every child must receive full-time education, from, at the latest, the term after their fifth birthday until, at the earliest, the end of the Easter term following their sixteenth birthday, if this is before the end of January, or on the Friday before the last Monday in May if the birthday falls between the end of January and 1 September. Under the Education Act 1980, parents may express a preference as to the school they wish their child to attend.

Every local education authority (LEA) has a team of education welfare officers (EWOs) part of whose responsibility is to follow up irregular attendance and to seek to improve it. The nature of the role and the status of EWOs varies markedly in different authorities; in some they perform and are recognized as sophisticated social workers within the educational system, while at the other extreme their role and status have not developed from that of the school attendance officer.

When there is concern about a child's school attendance, and informal efforts to improve it have failed, parents are served with a written notice of the LEA's intention to serve a school attendance order (Education Act 1944, s.37, as amended). The notice must specify the school it is intended to name in the order and may list suitable alternative schools. Parents may at this stage opt for the name of one of these, which will then be named in the order. Once the school attendance order is issued, the child's failure to attend the named school renders the parents liable to proceedings in the magistrates' court. Fines may be imposed for the first two offences and prison sentences of up to 1 month subsequently.

Education supervision orders

Under the Children Act care and supervision orders can no longer be sought on education grounds alone, as they could under the Children and Young Persons Act 1969 s.1(2)(e). Instead, whether or not the parents are proceeded against, the local education authority, having consulted with the local authority social services committee, may apply to the court for an education supervision order putting under their supervision a child of compulsory school age who is not being properly educated (Children Act 1989 s.36 and Schedule 3 Part III). The order requires the supervising officer to 'advise, assist and befriend and give directions to' the child and his parents, with the aim of ensuring that the child receives efficient full-time education suitable to his age ability and aptitude and any special educational needs that he may have.

Education supervision order proceedings are family proceedings under the Act which means that when a court is considering an application the child's welfare must be the paramount consideration, and the court is required only to make an order if it is satisfied that doing so would be better for the child than making no order. Guidance suggests that all possible efforts should have been made to resolve problems of poor school attendance before proceedings are begun. Courts will require detailed reports, the suggested contents of which are also contained in the Guidance (DoH (1991a) Vol. 7).

An order will cease to have effect after one year or when the child reaches school leaving age, but may be extended on application to the court for up to three years. The order is to the education authority and the supervisor will be an education welfare officer or education social worker. Paragraph 12 of Schedule 3 of the Act provides that directions attached to the order apply both to the child and to the parents, which includes anyone who is not a parent but has parental responsibility for the child, or anyone who is caring for the child. Persistent failure to comply with reasonable directions may constitute an offence, and supervising officers are under a duty to draw the attention of the court to the matter.

Where a parent or child persistently fails to comply with a direction given under the order the supervising officer is under a duty to inform the social services department who must investigate the child's circumstances and consider whether they should take any action, such as care proceedings under section 31, to secure the welfare of the child.

If parents choose to educate their children at home or to send them to a 'free' school (an independent school not registered as such by the Department of Education and Science), the LEA must satisfy itself that the provision is 'appropriate' and the onus of proof is on the parent. If the authority is not satisfied, it may issue a school attendance order.

Special educational needs

The Education Act 1981   Implemented in 1984, it is the legislative response to the *Report of the Committee of Enquiry into the Education of Handicapped Children and Young People*, chaired by Baroness Warnock (HMSO, 1978).

A child has special educational needs if he/she has a learning difficulty which requires special educational provision. Learning difficulty is defined as:

(a)   a significantly greater difficulty in learning than the majority of children of his age;
(b)   a disability which prevents him making use of educational facilities of the kind usually provided in school within the LEA for children of his age.

Any child under 5 years who is or would be likely to fall into either of the above categories on reaching school age unless special educational provision were made is defined as having special learning difficulties, although no child may be so regarded solely because the language or form of language used at any time at home is different from that used at school.

Special educational provision is defined as any educational provision for a child under 2 years of age, and that which is additional to, or different from, education provision in schools maintained by the LEA for children over 2 years. Interpretation of 'learning difficulty' is problematic and has resulted in several case decisions (Liell and Saunders, 1987).

When an LEA decides that a child needs assessment as to whether he/she has special educational needs, a notice must be served on the parents or guardian of that decision and the procedure that will be followed (1981 Act, s.5). If following the assessment the LEA decides that no special provision is required, the parents may appeal to the Secretary of State for

Education who has the power to direct the authority to reconsider, but he cannot direct them to act differently.

If the authority decides that special provision is required, it has to make a 'Statement' of the child's educational needs and is under a duty to 'arrange that special educational provision specified in the statement is made for him unless his parents make suitable arrangements' (s.7(2)).

The underlying philosophy of the Warnock Report and the basic strategy of the Act is that, wherever possible, special provision should be made within ordinary schools and only where this is not appropriate should children be sent to special schools. Parents wishing to appeal against the provision proposed for their child have to appeal first to an Appeal Committee which may confirm the decision or remit it to the LEA for reconsideration. A parent who is still not satisfied may appeal to the Secretary of State who at this stage has the power – very occasionally used – to direct the authority to make other provision.

Research into the working of the 1981 Act reveals a sad catalogue of long delays, blanket policies and failure to treat individual cases on their merits (Stone, 1987). Social workers have a key role to play in supporting parents in the exercise of the limited rights that they have under the Act. The relative powerlessness of parents in this procedure is underlined by the divisional court's ruling in *R.* v. *Hereford and Worcester County Council or Another, ex parte Lashford* [1987] that even if an LEA decides that a child has special educational needs, it has also a discretion as to whether or not special provision is required, and if it is decided that it is not, it cannot be compelled to make a Statement under s.7(1).

Welfare rights
The term 'welfare rights' is used here as meaning entitlement to payment of benefit from the state either on the basis of contributions paid or a particular status – childhood, old age or handicap – or entitlement for a variety of reasons to income support.

The legal framework of the provision of benefit is necessary to an understanding of the welfare rights system (however, the detailed working of the system, although an essential part of social work practice, is beyond the scope of an introductory text). Excellent up-to-date, detailed guidance on entitlement

Table 1   Classes of National Insurance Contribution

Class	Paid by:	Entitlement
1	Jointly by employed earners and their employers	All contributory benefits
2	Self-employed	All except unemployment
3	Voluntary contributions	Widows benefit and retirement pension
4	Self-employed with profits above prescribed level	None

and published annually by the Child Poverty Action Group (CPAG), the Disability Alliance and other organizations; useful wall-chart guides are also produced by *Community Care* and other social work publications. In order to make any sense of the tangled maze of available benefit, it may be helpful to consider the basic distinction between those benefits to which there is entitlement regardless of means and those which are means-tested. The non-means-tested social security benefits include all those towards which National Insurance Contributions are paid, together with those such as child benefit which are paid as of right without contribution or means-test. National welfare benefits are all income related and therefore means-tested. The two categories will be considered separately.

Non-means-tested social security benefits
National Insurance Contributions   There are four different classes of contributions paid on the basis of an 'earnings factor' by different categories of people between school-leaving and retirement age which give rise to varying entitlement to benefit (Table 1). A fixed percentage of all contributions goes towards funding the National Health Service and the rest towards national insurance benefits.

The principal benefits, excluding retirement and industrial injuries benefit, are:

1. *Unemployment benefit*   Payable after 3 days' unemployment to those who satisfy the contributions conditions

and sign on as available for work at the unemployment benefit office. Unemployment benefit is paid for a maximum of 312 days, after which there must be a further period of work before it can be reclaimed.

2. *Benefits for those incapable of work on medical grounds* Most employees who are away from work due to illness receive statutory sick pay (SSP) from their employers for the first 28 weeks; those who do not and have paid the appropriate contributions will be entitled to sickness benefit. After 28 weeks, there may be entitlement to invalidity benefit or, in certain circumstances, to severe disablement allowance. For all these benefits medical evidence will be required.

3. *Maternity benefit* Statutory maternity pay (SMP), now the main source of income for pregnant women, is the minimum maternity pay a woman who has worked continuously for the same employer for at least 6 months, and who satisfies the earnings conditions, is entitled to from her employer. Maternity allowance is payable to pregnant women who satisfy the employment requirements but are not entitled to statutory maternity pay.

4. *Widows benefit* Entitlement to benefit depends on the woman's husband's contributions, her age when widowed and whether she has dependent children (Cooper, 1990).

Non-contributory benefits relating to status or disability
Benefits for children Child benefit is payable for all children under school-leaving age, or aged 16–19 and in full-time education. Payment is made to a parent or other who is 'responsible' for the child, either because he/she lives as a child of the family or the parent pays at least the current rate of benefit for maintenance of the child.

The elderly Certain very elderly people who are not entitled to retirement and contribution-related pensions may be entitled to a small pension if they satisfy other conditions.

Benefits payable to the severely disabled
(a) *Mobility allowance (Social Security Act 1975, s.37A)* This is designed to help those between the ages of 5 and 65 (continuing to 75 for those already in receipt) who are unable, or virtually unable, to walk and are likely

to remain so for at least 12 months. It is not taxable and is disregarded in the assessment of resources for the principal means-tested benefits. Persons provided with an invalid carriage or adapted car are not also entitled to a mobility allowance, though they may transfer to that scheme or use their mobility allowance to buy or hire a car.

(b) *Attendance allowance (Social Security Act 1975, s.35 (1))*   A person is entitled to an attendance allowance if he/she satisfies the prescribed conditions as to residence and either

    (i)   is so severely disabled physically or mentally that, by day, requires from another person:

        – frequent attention throughout the day in connection with bodily functions, or

        – continual supervision throughout the day in order to avoid substantial danger to self or to others;

    (ii) is so severely disabled physically or mentally that, at night, requires from another person:

        – prolonged or repeated attention during the night in connection with bodily functions, or

        – continual supervision throughout the night in order to avoid substantial danger to self or to others.

Entitlement to an attendance allowance is determined by Adjudication Officers and the Attendance Allowance Board. The allowance may be payable at a higher or lower rate according to whether the disabled person needs the prescribed attention throughout the 24 hours or only by night or only by day. The allowance is not taxable, and not taken into account when entitlement to supplementary benefit is being assessed.

(c) *Invalid care allowance (Social Security Act 1975, s.37)*   Here provision is for an allowance for a claimant who can establish that he is engaged for at least 35 hours per week in caring for a severely disabled person in receipt of an attendance allowance or industrial injuries constant attendance allowance. A carer is not eligible for ICA if earning more than £30 per week from employment or in full-time eduation.

(For greater detail consult the DSS Guide HB5 and the Disability Alliance *Disability Rights Handbook*.)

Claims

Apart from unemployment benefit and family credit, all social security benefit claims will usually be dealt with, at least initially, by the DSS local office, where all inquiries should be made. Entitlement to most benefits depends on a claim being submitted on the appropriate DSS form, usually provided with the booklet describing the particular benefit. Although a limited amount of backdating is possible, those who may be entitled to benefit should be encouraged to claim at once as there are strict time limits which can only be extended 'for good cause'.

Most initial decisions on claims are taken by the Adjudication Officer, who should reach a decision within 14 days. Undue delay may be grounds for complaint to the Ombudsman. When the Adjudication Officer has reached a decision, a dissatisfied applicant can appeal in writing to a social security appeal tribunal made up of a legally qualified chairperson and two others. The Child Poverty Action Group (CPAG) provide detailed advice on the conduct of appeals.

National welfare income-related benefits

The Social Security Act 1986 introduced major changes in the main income-related benefits and, in particular, to the single payments scheme for exceptional needs now replaced with discretionary payments from the social fund, most in the form of loans. This book can only offer an outline guide to the legal basis of provision; details of entitlement and procedures for claiming are set out in detail and with great clarity (considering the complexity) in CPAG's annually published *National Welfare Benefits Handbook*.

The three main income-related benefits are Income Support (IS) for those not in full-time work; Family Credit (FC) for those in low-paid employment; and Housing Benefit (HB) to help with the payment of rent and rates.

Income Support is intended to be the safety net of the welfare state. Anyone who has capital of less than £6,000 and is not in full-time work (24 hours or more a week), and whose partner is not in full-time work and whose income drops below the level laid down annually by Parliament, is, provided that certain conditions are satisfied, entitled to have his/her income brought up to the IS level.

The general conditions that have to be satisfied by claimants for IS relate to age, residence and work. Entitlement to IS is calculated on the basis of the applicable amount for the claimant, partner and children according to their age, less any deductions for income or capital (£3,000–£6,000), plus any premiums payable in recognition of age, ill-health or other additional family responsibilities (Cooper, 1990).

Those in receipt of IS will also be entitled to HB (see below). Claimants living in special sorts of accommodation, such as residential care or board and lodging accommodation, have their IS calculated on the basis of an amount for personal expenses and an allowance towards the costs of accommodation. Claims for IS are made to local DSS offices, and decisions are reached by adjudication officers and may be appealed against to social security appeal tribunals.

Family Credit replaced Family Income Supplement for families in low-paid work in April 1988. It is paid to couples and single parents with dependent children when the claimant or partner works 24 hours or more each week, meets the residence requirements and has capital of less than £6,000. The amount of FC paid depends on the size of the family, their income and any capital between £3,000 and £6,000 for which deductions are made.

Claims for FC are made to the DSS on the form accompanying the leaflet FC1 obtaining from those offices, or most post offices. Unlike IS, all claims are processed centrally by the Family Credit Unit at Blackpool, although appeals against miscalculation or refusal of FC lie to a social security appeal tribunal.

Those in receipt of FC are not entitled to IS, but may qualify for HB and, as with those on IS, for help in the future towards payment of the Community Charge. Receipt of IS or FC will, in many circumstances, entitle claimants to additional medical and educational benefits and to legal aid.

Housing Benefit   is a national scheme run by local authorities designed to help people on low incomes, whether married or single and with or without children, to pay their rent and rates. The legal framework of the scheme is set out in the Social Security Act 1986, Part II. The very complex law and regulations with an expert commentary can be found in

CPAG's *Annotated Housing Benefit Legislation 1988/89* and in publications by housing pressure groups. Housing law is constantly being developed by judicial decison; reports of important cases with commentary are published in *Legal Action*, the montly bulletin of the Legal Action Group.

Claims for HB have to be made in writing to the local authority, unless the claimant is already claiming IS, in which case claims may be directed either to the authority or the DHSS who forward them. Although the law is complex, the basic principles of HB calculations are simple; their application is again made clear by CPAG's step-by-step guide.

The local authority should reach a decision on HB within 14 days of receiving a valid claim and must notify the applicant in writing. Dissatisfied applicants may ask for a more detailed explanation and an internal review by an HB officer on the basis of written comments on the decision. Beyond this, there is no independent appeal tribunal, although the applicant may put his case to a review board made up of three local councillors (Cooper, 1990).

The Social Fund
Death and maternity grants paid regardless of income and additional payments of supplementary benefit for special expenses were abolished by the 1986 Act and replaced with grants from the Social Fund payable on a non-discretionary basis for funeral, maternity and severe weather payments (hopefully), and on a highly controversial discretionary basis for exceptional needs payments.

Payments from the non-discretionary Social Fund depend on eligibility through current entitlement to IS, FC or HB. The cash-limited Social Fund provides for budgeting loans which are repayable, and community care grants which are not. Budgeting loans may be made to claimants on IS for a variety of immediate needs. Community care grants are intended to help with the re-establishment of those leaving residential care or to help prevent the need for a move into care. The experience of those who have assisted claimants suggests that considerable help with form-filling and perseverance in pursuing claims is necessary. Claims for loans or grants have to be made to Social Fund Officers (SFOs) in DSS offices, who reach their decisions on the basis of the law, 'directions' issued by the Secretary of State which must be followed and 'guidance' which SFOs must take account of. Extracts from this 'guidance' are included in CPAG's *National Welfare Benefits Handbook*. A dissatisfied claimant has the right to ask for review by the SFO who made the decision, and if still dissatisfied, to a further review by a Social Fund Inspector. There is no right of appeal to a tribunal (Cooper, 1990).

Discrimination

Discrimination exists in many forms. It is legislated against only in the areas of race and sex, and the effectiveness of existing legislation is frequently called into question. The Race Relations Act 1976, and the Sexual Discrimination Act 1975, make very similar provision by making overtly discriminatory behaviour a criminal offence and by setting up the Commission for Racial Equality and Equal Opportunities Commission to monitor the legislation and encourage good practice. Legislation in this field is a blunt instrument, the limitation of which is manifestly apparent. (Detailed examination of the legislation and its application to particular situations is beyond the scope of this book and reference should be made to specialist tests, Lustgarten, 1980; Pannick, 1985.)

3 The criminal process

The police and their powers

The Police and Criminal Evidence Act 1984 provides a statutory framework within which the police must operate when investigating crime; most of the Act was implemented in January 1986. It replaces provisions in several statutes, and most importantly, the 'Judges' Rules', a series of administrative directions which previously regulated police interviews and the evidence obtained from interrogation. The Act finally reached the statute-book after several years of official inquiries, evidence taken from interested parties, two Bills and the longest – and one of the most acrimonious – Parliamentary debates over major legislation in recent years. Experience of Police and Criminal Evidence Act 1984 (PACE) procedures is resulting in a continuing police and civil liberties debate, especially over the right to silence.

The law is contained in the Act, supported by four critically important Codes of Practice, which while they are not law, have a higher status than the 'Judges' Rules', in that although a breach of the Codes cannot itself be made the subject of criminal proceedings or the foundation of a civil action for damages, any breach is an automatic breach of police discipline and therefore may be the subject of disciplinary proceedings. The Codes were substantially revised in 1990 (Zander, 1990).

The Codes of Practice provide an elaborate system of rules for dealing with suspects:

31

(a)   stop and search;
(b)   search of premises and seizure;
(c)   detention, treatment and questioning;
(d)   identification of suspects;
(e)   tape recording.

In a trial the defence will be able to refer to a breach of the Code, but evidence obtained in breach will not automatically be excluded, although a recent Court of Appeal decision shows that its admission may be grounds for appeal if a 'guilty' verdict was rendered unsafe (*R.* v. *Delany* [1988]). The test in relation to confessions – the most critical area – has been considerably altered by section 76 of the Act. The old test of the confession only being admissible if it was not obtained 'by oppression' and if 'voluntary' has been altered. The 1984 Act retains the exclusion of evidence obtained by 'oppression' which is defined, but it replaces the old test of whether the confession had been obtained by 'fear of prejudice or hope of advantage' with one which questions whether anything said or done at the time at which the confession was made was likely 'in the circumstances existing at the time, to render unreliable any confession which might be made ... in consequence thereof' (*R.* v. *Delany* [1988]). As a measure of protection for the defendant, the statute firmly puts the burden of proof that the confession is not 'unreliable' on the prosecution.

The Act also introduced considerable changes in relation to the evidence that spouses may, or may be compelled, to give evidence for or against each other (Zander, 1990). Under the provisions of section 80, spouses are competent and compellable witnesses for the accused unless they are jointly charged. They are competent witnesses for the prosecution in all cases and may be compelled if the case involves violence against the other spouse or against anyone who was under 16 years at the time of the offence, or where the offence was a sexual one against anyone under 16 years (s.80(3)).

'Stop and search'
Under section 1 of the Act, police officers are given the power to search any 'person or vehicle' and 'anything which is in or on a vehicle, for stolen or prohibited articles' and to detain a person or vehicle for the purpose of such a search, provided that there are 'reasonable grounds' for suspecting that stolen

or prohibited articles will be found. These include offensive weapons or articles made or adapted for use in burglary, theft, taking a motor vehicle or obtaining property by deception.

The Code defines both 'suspicion' and 'reasonable grounds' restrictively: 'Reasonable suspicion, in contrast to mere suspicion, must be founded on fact. There must be some concrete basis for the officer's belief, related to the person concerned, which can be considered and evaluated by an objective third person.' The notes of guidance accompanying the revised Code A emphasize the fact that misuse of police powers is likely to lead to mistrust of the police by the community. The power to stop and search can be exercised in any place to which the public, or a section of the public, have access but not when people or their cars are on their own private land, or on private land on which they have specific permission to be. Searches on those premises require a search warrant.

The Act (s.2) lays down procedural safeguards to prevent abuse of the power to stop and search. These involve the police having to identify themselves and provide the owner of a vehicle with a written record of the search. The person searched must be detained for no longer than the search takes (Cooper, 1990).

Powers of entry, search and seizure
Warrants to *enter and search premises* for evidence of serious arrestable offences are issued on application to a Justice of the Peace. The application must give reasonable grounds for believing that the offence has been committed, and there is material on the premises likely to be of value and relevant to the investigation, which is not 'excluded', or 'special procedure material, and that access to the premises is impracticable without a warrant. Warrants to search for records held on confidential files, medical samples and some journalistic material can only be granted by circuit judges (Police and Criminal Evidence Act 1984, s.9).

Arrest
Arrest may be lawfully effected in a number of ways, depending on the seriousness of the offences.

Arrest by the police without a warrant
Where a constable has reasonable grounds for suspecting that
an arrestable offence has been committed, he may arrest without warrant

1.   anyone whom he has reasonable grounds for suspecting
     to be guilty of an offence;
2.   anyone who is about to commit; or
3.   anyone whom he has reasonable grounds to suspect to be
     about to commit an arrestable offence (s.24);
4.   anyone who has within the previous month been con-
     victed of a recordable offence, for which he was not held
     in police custody, for the purpose of taking his finger-
     prints if he has failed to comply within 7 days to a request
     to attend a police station for this purpose (s.27).

The power of arrest for arrestable offences applies

1.   to offences for which the penalty is fixed by law (e.g.
     murder and treason);
2.   to offences carrying a penalty of 5 or more years' impri-
     sonment;
3.   to offences in subsection 2 – some fairly serious offences
     which were not previously arrestable.

General arrest conditions (s.25)   All other offences carry a
limited power of arrest if a constable has reasonable grounds
for suspecting that any offence has been committed or
attempted, or is being committed or attempted, and it appears
to him that service of a summons is impracticable or inappropriate because any of the 'general arrest conditions' is satisfied. These are that:

(a)   The officer does not know and cannot readily obtain the
      name and address of the suspect, or he reasonably
      believes them to be false, or he doubts whether the sus-
      pect has given an adequate address for service of a sum-
      mons.
(b)   These are reasonable grounds for believing that the
      arrest is necessary to prevent the suspect causing:

      –   physical harm to himself or to someone else;
      –   loss of or damage to property;

- an unlawful obstruction of the highway;
- an offence against public decency where the public cannot easily avoid the person to be arrested;
- to protect the child 'or other vulnerable person from the person to be arrested'.

An arrested person must be told at once, or as soon as is practicable, that he is under arrest and the grounds – even if these may be obvious.

Arrest under warrant   An arrest warrant may be issued by a justice of the peace for a serious offence where the offender is unlikely to, or has failed to answer, a summons.

Citizen's arrest   Any person has a right to arrest without warrant anyone who is committing, or is reasonably suspected of having committed, an offence. This right has not been affected by the Act.

Detention
Where a person attends voluntarily at a police station to assist with an investigation 'he shall be entitled to leave at will unless he is placed under arrest' (s.29), and where a person is arrested anywhere other than in a police station, the Act provides that he should be taken to a police station 'as soon as is practicable'. If there is a delay, the reasons for this must be recorded. Detention in a police station must be in conformity with the provisions of the Act and the custody officer, who will usually be of the rank of sergeant or above and should not be involved in the investigation, must order the release of anyone whose continued detention by the police cannot be justified under the Act.

Rights of an arrested person to information
As soon as practicable after arrival at the police station or after his arrest there, an arrested person must be told

1.   of the grounds of his detention;
2.   of the right to have someone informed;
3.   of the right to consult a copy of the Codes;
4.   of the right to legal advice.

Duties of the custody officer

The Act lays down that it is the duty of the custody officer to ensure that a person brought to a police station is charged if there is enough evidence to charge him, or released if there is not, unless there are reasonable grounds for believing that his detention is needed to preserve or obtain evidence of the offence for which he was arrested (s.37). As soon as is practicable, the custody officer must make a written record of the grounds of detention, preferably in the presence of the suspect who must be told of the grounds. The need for further detention must be reviewed by a review officer, of at least the rank of inspector, who has not been involved in the investigation, after 6 hours and thereafter at 9-hourly intervals. If the police wish to hold the suspect without putting charges after 24 hours, authorization must be given by a superintendent, or officer above, after hearing representations from the suspect or his solicitor, and after 36 hours approval must be obtained from a magistrates' court. The court can approve a further 36 hours (twice) up to an absolute maximum of 96 hours. There is limited provision in the Act for flexible interpretation of the time limits.

Questioning and treatment of persons by the police

The Custody Officer must take charge of searches of detained persons and make an inventory of the suspect's property. There may only be a search if the officer considers it necessary to make a complete list of his property, and a suspect may only be searched by a constable of the same sex. If a strip search is considered necessary, the reason must be recorded.

Intimate searches are allowed only if authorized by a superintendent or above, on the grounds of reasonable belief that the arrested person might have concealed anything that could be used to cause injury to himself or others, and that he might so use it, and that it could only be discovered by such a search.

When a person is under arrest in a police station, he is entitled, if he so requests, 'to have one friend or relative or other person who is known to him and likely to take an interest in his welfare' told as soon as is practicable that he is under arrest and his whereabouts (s.56).

Legal advice

An arrested person who is held in custody at a police station or other premises has the right to consult a solicitor privately at any time (Police and Criminal Evidence Act 1984 s.58). An interview should not begin without legal advice except in exceptional circumstances set out in the section (Levenson and Fairweather, 1990). The 24-hour duty solicitor scheme should ensure that legal advice is readily available, however in some areas worrying numbers of solicitors have withdrawn from the scheme.

Juveniles and other vulnerable groups

There are statutory safeguards designed to protect vulnerable groups, such as juveniles and the mentally disordered or those with learning disabilities, in interview situations and to minimize the risk of interviews producing unreliable evidence. When a child (10–13) or a young person (14–16) is arrested the police should inform the child's parent, guardian or other responsible person, including the local authority if the juvenile is in care, of the reason for the arrest and the place of detention. If there is an existing supervision order the supervisor must also be given the same information as soon as is reasonably practicable. Although under the Criminal Justice Act 1991 seventeen-year-olds will be treated as 'young persons' within the jurisdiction of the youth court, for interview (and remand) purposes they continue to be treated as adults, unless they come within one of the other vulnerable groups.

The 'appropriate adult' is defined as a parent or guardian, or if in care the care authority or voluntary organization worker, or a social worker, or failing any of those persons anyone over the age of 18 who is not a police officer or employed by the police. An estranged parent should not be asked to act as appropriate adult if the juvenile objects.

No interview with a juvenile or a mentally disordered person, or one with a learning disability, should take place without an appropriate adult being present unless the interview is extremely urgent in which case the reasons must be recorded in writing and the interview only cover the matters of urgency (Code C, Annex C). Code C para 11.16 provides that the appropriate adult should be informed that he or she is not expected to act merely as an observer, but has an active role to play: advising the person being questioned; observing whether or not the interview is being conducted fairly; and facilitating communication. Copies of all the Codes must be available for consultation.

Caution and charge

The Code C on Detention, Treatment and Questioning provides that a person whom there are grounds for suspecting of an offence must be cautioned before any questions, or further questions, are put to him for the purpose of obtaining evidence which may be given to a court in a prosecution. The caution must be in the following terms: 'You do not have to say anything unless you wish to do so, but what you say may be given in evidence'. Under Annex D of Code C there are detailed requirements relating to written records of interviews (*R*. v. *Delaney* [1988]). A new Code of Practice, E, sets out the procedures to be followed when interviews at a police station are recorded on tape. The Code is accompanied by detailed notes of guidance to police officers.

When a detained person has been charged, or a person has been informed that he may be prosecuted for an offence, he should be cautioned again. A charged person should be given written details of the offence, the police officer's name and the police station. After the charge is made, questions relating to the offence may not be put, with the exception of those necessary to minimize harm to others, or to clear up an ambiguity. Before any such questions the caution should be administered again.

Fingerprints should only be taken with consent, but may be taken without consent if a superintendent, or officer above, authorizes it on the grounds of reasonable suspicion of the involvement of that person in an offence and that his fingerprints will tend to confirm or disprove his involvement. In the case of juveniles under 17 years, a parent must consent for a child under 14, and both the parent and the young person where they are aged 14–16. A social worker representing the local authority can give consent for a child in care (Home Office, 1985).

Bail

A person is bailed when he is released from custody to attend at court or at a police station at a specific time. The primary purpose of bail is to secure the attendance of the defendant at court. Failure to attend constitutes a further offence (Bail Act 1976, s.6(1)).

If the police charge a detained person, they must release him on bail unless his name and address cannot be ascertained or are believed on reasonable grounds to be false. They may also detain in custody to appear in court within 36 hours those whom they believe are likely to harm others or themselves, or need protection, as well as those they consider unlikely to answer bail or likely to interfere with witnesses or police investigations (Zander, 1990).

When a defendant appears in court following arrest, or when a serious case is unfinished, the court has to decide whether to remand the defendant in custody or release him on bail. The provisions of the Bail Act 1976, which were intended to avoid unnecessary remands in custody, have been criticized both for failing to achieve that and, at the other end of the spectrum, for allowing the release on bail of serious offenders who commit further grave offences. These are currently under review. The presumption under the Act is that bail will be granted unless there are substantial grounds, which must be entered on the court record, for believing that the defendant if released would fail to surrender, commit further offences, interfere with witnesses or otherwise obstruct the course of justice. All the evidence suggests that there is a very wide discrepancy in the way that courts interpret these provisions (Bottomley, 1973). Bail may be granted unconditionally or subject to conditions imposed to ensure that any of the above grounds which might justify custody are avoided.

Trial venue

All criminal proceedings begin in the magistrates' court and over 90 per cent are concluded there. Magistrates have sole jurisdiction over all summary offences, but none over the most serious offences which are triable only on indictment; they may hear the substantial range of cases that can be tried 'either way' (Criminal Law Act 1977, s.19). If the case is triable on an indictment or is triable either way and the defendant elects jury trial, or the magistrates decide that their maximum sentence of £2,000 and/or 6 months' imprisonment would not be adequate, the defendant will be committed for trial either on bail or remanded in custody. Detailed accounts of the criminal trial, the process of sentencing and of the range of sentences available to the magistrates and the Crown Court are major topics well covered elsewhere (Stone, 1991(a) and (b); Wasik and Taylor, 1991).

PART II
CHILDREN AND
FAMILIES

Introduction to the Children Act 1989

When introducing the Children Bill into the House of Lords in November 1988 the Lord Chancellor, Lord Mackay referred to it as 'the most comprehensive and far reaching reform of child law which has come before Parliament in living memory'. In the first edition of this work and elsewhere the major shortcomings of child care law, and the court system in which it was administered, prior to implementation of the Children Act 1989, have been reviewed together with the progress of the reform process up to that date (Ball 1990). The passage of the Bill through Parliament was largely uncontentious and the period of nearly two years preparing for implementation allowed for (varying amounts of) consultation on guidance, rules and regulations made under the Act, and training for all the many professional groups and others affected by its implementation.

The Children Act 1989 not only comprises a comprehensive and coherent package of provisions operating within a set of clearly expressed principles, it also for the first time brings together the so-called public (the state's provision for child care and protection) and private law (orders relating to children made in proceedings between adult parties, i.e. following divorce) within a single statute. All court decisions are subject to the same welfare criteria, and most orders under the Act are available in all proceedings. The magistrates' family proceedings court, the county court and the High Court have concurrent jurisdiction to deal with all proceedings under the Act (Figure 1).

As the Lord Chancellor reiterated throughout the passage of the Bill through Parliament, and during the period of preparation for its implementation, although each of its twelve parts relate to different aspects of child law it must be read as a whole. The 'whole' meaning not only the Act, but also the mass of accompanying court rules, regulations and guidance which make the provisions workable. The relative status of regulations and guidance and their practice relevance is very helpfully explored in *Principles and Practice in Regulations and Guidance* (DoH, 1989b). Guidance and the relevant rules and regulations are published by the Department of Health in nine volumes covering all the public law (DoH (1991a) Vols 1–9).

Origins, principles and proceedings

Apart from the overall need to provide a clear and balanced statutory framework for child care practice, the private law provisions of the 1989 Act are informed by the painstaking work of the Law Commission (Law Commission, 1985, 1986, 1987a, 1987b and 1988) and the public law by the Review of Child Care Law (RCCL, 1985), the Report of the Committee of Inquiry into Child Abuse in Cleveland (Butler-Sloss, 1988), and the findings of the massive body of research evidence commissioned in the late 1970s and published from 1985 onwards (DHSS, 1985). The findings of these studies demonstrated in a variety of ways the damaging effects of the poor child care practice which flourished within legal provisions which allowed, or even encouraged, resort to statutory orders rather than cooperation with parents (Packman *et al.*, 1986; Vernon and Fruin, 1986). The daunting legal disadvantage of parents when trying to challenge local authorities' decisions – particularly over contact with their children in care – resulted in too many children leaving care having lost all contact with their birth families (Millham *et al.*, 1986), and, particularly apparent in Cleveland, the voices of the children being too often ignored when they should have been listened to (Butler-Sloss, 1988).

The 1989 Act is grounded on the belief that children are best brought up by their own parents with the courts and the state only intervening where absolutely necessary. The concept of parental responsibility replaces the term parental rights and duties, and gives statutory weight to children's rights, both in regard to having their wishes and feelings consulted whenever decisions about their future is made, and, if considered to be of sufficient age and understanding, being able to refuse medical examination or assessment. The changes to the so-called private law relating to children, that which concerns orders relating to children made in proceedings such as divorce, contained in Part II of the Act, seek to encourage the continued involvement of both parents in their children's upbringing, regardless of the ending of their relationship with each other.

The public law provisions of the Children Act were drafted with the intention of securing a better balance between the rights of children to have their voice heard, the rights of parents to bring up their children without interference, and the duty of the state as represented by local authorities, supported by the courts, to intervene where a child's welfare requires it. Getting that balance right presents one of the most difficult tasks that legislators face. For nearly half a century attempts have been made to achieve this balance by means of piecemeal measures to correct perceived swings too far in one or other direction, which often subsequently proved to be over corrections (Rowe, 1989). Only practice experience and research evidence will demonstrate whether or not the Children Act 1989 succeeds where past attempts have failed.

The principles that underpin the Act are that:

i) children are generally best looked after within the family, with both parents playing a full part in their upbringing, helped when necessary by the local authority;
ii) children's voices should be listened to;
iii) court proceedings should be a last resort;
iv) in any court proceedings the child's welfare is the court's paramount consideration;
v) delay by courts in reaching decisions is likely to be damaging to the child;
vi) in most proceedings courts should consider the whole range of available orders and not only those applied for, and that;
vii) they should only make orders which are likely to be of positive benefit to the child.

The range of orders now available in family proceedings give the courts a flexibility previously only available in wardship. A marked feature of this is that the private law orders – residence, contact, specific issues and prohibited steps, set out in section 8, and family assistance orders under section 16, may be made in care and other proceedings, whether or not they are applied for (DoH (1991a) Vol. 1). For instance a court considering a local authority application for a care or supervision order may, if that is what they consider to be in the child's best interests, make a residence order to a relative or friend instead.

4 Parents, guardians and parental responsibility

The concept of parental responsibility rather than parental rights is central to the philosophy of the Children Act 1989. (Eekelaar and Dingwall, 1990). The law relating to the acquisition of parental responsibility, previously found in various statutes is clarified and in important respects altered. Parents married to each other at the time of the child's birth, or subsequently, have joint parental responsibility which can only be terminated by death or by the adoption of the child. An unmarried father is a parent of the child in law, but he can only acquire parental responsibility by formal written agreement with the child's mother, or by court order (Children Act 1989 s.4).

Guardians

The legal guardian of a child has full parental responsibility in the place of a parent. Anyone may apply to the court to become the guardian of an orphan child, or a child in respect of whom a residence order was made to a parent who died whilst the order was in force. The power to appoint a guardian to assume the place of the parent in the event of his or her death is one which can only be exercised by a parent with parental responsibility. If such a parent dies his or her appointment in writing of a guardian will only take immediate effect if the child has no other parent with parental responsibility living, or if the parent who died had a residence order in regard to the child at the time of death. Otherwise the appointment will not take effect unless the other parent dies whilst the child is still a minor (Children Act 1989 s.5).

Non-parents
Parental responsibility may be acquired by non-parents:

i)   Any person who has a residence order in their favour has parental responsibility for the child as long as the order lasts.
ii)   a local authority has parental responsibility when the child is the subject of a care order, or for the duration of an emergency protection order.

Parents do not lose their responsibility as a consequence of any other acquiring a residence order or the child being made the subject of a care order, but the power to exercise important aspects of it – such as determining where the child shall live – will be curtailed.

   Adoption effects a complete legal transfer of a child from the birth family to the adoptive family. The adoption order vests parental responsibility in the adopters and brings to an end that of the birth parents.

5 Family breakdown

When a marriage breaks down, the relief sought will largely determine the nature of the legal proceedings. Permanent dissolution of a valid marriage, when both parties are still living, can be achieved only by divorce proceedings, though a marriage suffering from a fundamental defect, such as non-consummation, may be annulled. In other proceedings orders may be made which relate to the parties or children of a marriage or, in some circumstances, to cohabitees. The law relating to marriage and the family is both wide in its scope and complex in nature; this chapter gives only a brief introduction; for further detail it will be necessary to consult a specialist textbook (Cretney and Masson, 1990).

Divorce

A marriage can be terminated only by death or by a decree of divorce or nullity. All suits for divorce are commenced by a petition presented to a divorce county court, and almost all will be concluded there; cases may be transferred to the High Court if their complexity, difficulty or gravity justify the move (Practice Direction 1987).

Legal aid was withdrawn from almost all undefended divorce proceedings in 1977, although it is available to make or oppose an application for an injunction, financial relief or an order in relation to children. Petitioners have therefore to draft their own petition and take all the further steps, or pay a solicitor. If petitioners qualify financially, they may be entitled to free legal advice under the 'green-form' scheme up to £90 in value which could provide assistance with form-filling. Printed forms of petition are available from law stationers and court staff are also helpful to unrepresented parties.

No petition may be presented within the first year of marriage, though one presented after that may be based on events which occurred during the first year. Under the Matrimonial Causes Act 1973, the sole ground for divorce is that the marriage has irretrievably broken down; this can only be established by proving one of the five grounds set out in section 1 of the Act:

1. that the respondent has committed adultery and that the petitioner finds it intolerable to live with the respondent;
2. that the respondent has behaved in such a way that the petitioner cannot be expected to live with the respondent;
3. that the respondent has deserted the petitioner; and that this has been for a continuous period of 2 years;
4. that the parties have lived apart for a continuous period of at least 2 years, and that the respondent consents to the decree being granted;
5. that the parties have lived apart for a continuous period of at least 5 years immediately preceding the presentation of the petition.

Although the consent of the respondent is not required, the decree may be withheld if it can be shown that to grant it would cause grave financial or other hardship.

When the petition is served on the respondent, it must be accompanied by two forms, one sets out the steps to be taken and the consequences of a decree and the other is a form of acknowledgement of service which asks the respondent whether the proceedings are going to be defended. If the respondent wishes to defend the proceedings, he/she must file an answer within 29 days of receiving the petition and then the case will be heard in open court.

Under what is called the 'special procedure' – in fact the normal procedure in undefended cases – neither party needs attend court. The petitioner has to make a written application for directions for trial accompanied by an affidavit verifying the facts set out in the petition, any corroborative evidence relied on and certain other information. The district judge enters the cause in the special procedure list and, provided that he is satisfied that the petitioner has proved his/her case and is entitled to a decree, this will be certified and a date fixed on which the judge will announce the decree nisi in open court.

Unless the court order to the contrary the petitioner may apply after 6 weeks (or any shorter time fixed by the court) for the decree to be made absolute. If the petitioner does not apply, the respondent may do so after 3 months from the earliest date on which the petitioner could have applied. Once the decree is absolute (but not before), the marriage is at an end and either party may remarry.

In addition to granting the divorce decree, the court may make a wide range of orders regarding finance, property and where necessary, children. The court no longer has to certify that it is satisfied with the arrangements made for the children of the family. Instead the new section 41 of the Matrimonial Causes Act 1973 (Child Act 1989 Schedule 12 para. 31) provides that the court shall consider whether it should exercise any of its powers under the Act. If it considers that an order may be necessary, but is not in a position to decide, it must declare that the decree may not be made absolute until the court so orders.

Children of the family

The whole principle and nature of orders regarding the children of the family following the breakdown of a marriage have been profoundly altered by the Children Act 1989. Under the private law provisions of that Act both parents will, following divorce, continue to have parental responsibility for their children regardless of the breakdown of their relationship. If they are able to agree about the children's future it is assumed that they will both have an equal say in their children's future and there is no need for any court order. Each parent will continue to exercise 'all the rights, duties, powers, responsibilities and authority which by law a parent of a child has in relation to the child and his property' (Children Act 1989 s.3(1)).

The welfare criteria

All cases involving decisions regarding the care and upbringing of children and the administration of their property are subject to s.1(1) of the Act:

the child's welfare shall be the court's paramount consideration.

In most proceedings courts have to consider each of the items set out in the welfare checklist in section 1(3) in order to make an informed decision. This requires the court to have regard 'in particular to:

a)   the ascertainable wishes and feelings of the child concerned (considered in the light of his age and understanding);
b)   his physical educational and emotional needs;
c)   the likely effect on him of any change in his circumstances;
d)   his age, sex, background and any characteristics of his which the court considers relevant;
e)   any harm which he has suffered or is at risk of suffering;
f)   how capable each of his parents, and any other person in relation to whom the court considers the question to be relevant, is of meeting his needs;
g)   the range of powers available to the court under this Act in the proceedings in question.'

Section 8 orders
Where parents are not able to agree, or others wish to be involved either by caring for or having contact with the child, the Act provides, in section 8, a menu of orders none of which remove parental responsibility although they may to a lesser or greater extent restrict its exercise. The section 8 orders are:

'Residence orders' settle the arrangements as to the person with whom the child is to live.

'Contact orders' which require the person with whom the child lives to allow the child to visit or stay with the person named in the order or otherwise (i.e. by letter, phone, photographs, etc.) to have contact with him.

'Prohibited steps orders' under which steps might be taken by a parent in meeting parental responsibility, but which are specified in the order, may not be taken without leave of the court.

'Specific issues orders' give directions regarding a particular question in connection with any aspect of parental responsibility.

Section 8 orders are available in most family proceedings under the Act as well as divorce proceedings. Parents, including unmarried fathers, guardians and anyone who has a residence order in their favour may apply as of right for any section 8 order, except that no application for a section 8 order apart from a residence order may be made in regard to a child who is the subject of a care order (see p. 73). The right to apply for a residence or contact order without leave is restricted to:

i)   Any party to a marriage (whether or not subsisting) in relation to whom the child is a 'child of the family' as defined in section 105(1):
'(a) a child of both those parties;
(b) any other child, not being a child who is placed with those parties by a local authority or voluntary organization, who has been treated by both those parties as a child or their family';

ii) any person with whom the child has lived for a period of at least three years within the previous five years;

iii) any person who has obtained the necessary consents (s.10(5)).

All other persons including children concerned in the proceedings require the leave of the court before they can apply, and local authority foster parents and those who have fostered a child within the previous six months additionally require the prior permission of the local authority, unless they are relatives of the child (s.9(3) and (4)).

When deciding whether to grant leave courts have to have regard to the nature of the proposed application; the applicant's connection with the child, and the likely effect, in terms of disruption to the child's life, of the application. At the leave stage although the welfare test must be applied the court does not have to consider the child's wishes and feelings or the other 'checklist' items.

Family assistance order
Under section 16 of the Children Act 1989 in family proceedings, with the consent of the parties, courts may make a family assistance order for up to six months. This order is intended to provide short-term help from a probation officer or local authority social worker to 'advise and assist and (where appropriate) befriend members of a family'. The main purpose of the order is to provide help in the immediate aftermath of family breakdown, in particular help over contact arrangements, etc. Unless there is a concurrent section 8

order the supervisor has no power to bring the section 16 order back to court for a variation (DoH (1991a) Vol. 1 para 2.50).

Financial provision

Under section 1 of the Magistrates' Courts and Domestic Proceedings Act 1978, a spouse (usually the wife) whose husband has failed to maintain her and the children properly, or has behaved in such a way that she cannot be expected to live with him, or has deserted her, can seek:

(a) an order making financial provision;
(b) the court's approval of agreed arrangements;
(c) confirmation of a level of payment which has been made voluntarily for the past 3 months.

The order may be both for periodical and lump-sum payments (not exceeding £1000).

In advance of implementation of the Child Support Act, 1991 under which a Child Support Agency will become responsible for the assessment and collection of maintenance payments in respect of children, the courts have been given considerably enhanced powers under the Maintenance Enforcement Act 1991 aimed at improving payment of maintenance orders for spouses and children.

Jurisidiction in private law proceedings

The magistrates' family proceedings court has a concurrent jurisdiction with the county court and the High Court in most private law proceedings relating to family breakdown under the Children Act 1989, and sole jurisdiction in what remains of the Magistrates Courts and Domestic Proceedings Act 1978. Magistrates have no jurisdiction in divorce or wardship proceedings. For those who qualify financially assistance by way of representation through the legal aid scheme covers the cost of a solicitor preparing a case and representing a party in most private law cases in the family proceedings court.

The matrimonial home

1. *Ownership* and rights on dissolution of a marriage are technical, complex and beyond the scope of this book; for a lucid explanation, see Cretney and Masson (1990, ch. 10).

2.   *Occupation*   It is often the right to occupy the matrimonial or joint home that is critical at the time a relationship breaks down. If both spouses or partners have a beneficial interest in the home, for instance, as co-owners or joint tenants, they have equal rights of occupation. If only one has a beneficial interest, the position of a spouse without legal title is more secure than that of a cohabitee, who none the less may have some protection; each need separate consideration.

Spouse's right to occupy a home, in which only one spouse has a legal title   Under section (1) of the Matrimonial Homes Act 1983, it is stated:

> Where one spouse is entitled to occupy a dwelling house ... and the other spouse is not so entitled ... the spouse not so entitled shall have the following rights of occupation:
>
> (a)   if in occupation, a right not to be evicted or excluded from the dwelling house or any part thereof except with the leave of the court given by an order under this section;
> (b)   if not in occupation, a right with the leave of the court so given to enter into and occupy the dwelling house.

The applicant spouse's rights under the Act are dependent on:

(i)   the marriage still being in existence;
(ii)   the entitled spouse having a legal right to occupy.

Cohabitee's right to occupy   A cohabitee without legal title may be protected if they can establish:

(i)   a contractual licence, by virtue of an interest they may have given up which may amount to consideration;
(ii)   a licence by estoppel if the other party has acted in such a way as to be estopped from denying the existence of the right of occupancy;
(iii) otherwise a cohabitee will only have a bare licence and the owner of the premises may recover possession after giving reasonable notice to quit.

Excluding a party from occupation   For this, see below, p. 56.

Domestic violence
Legal protection for victims of domestic violence whether
adults or children is contained in a hotchpotch of statutory
provision. The Children Act 1989 parts IV and V provides for
state intervention to protect children who have suffered or are
at risk from both parents (see Chapter 7). The protection of
partners, and of children for whom one partner could provide
a safe home if the other were excluded, are dealt with in a
piecemeal manner in a number of statutes under which varying remedies are available and criteria apply. The main issues
are accommodation and personal protection (Freeman, 1987).

Accommodation
Under the Housing Act 1985, Part III (Homeless Persons), a
person who has left accommodation as a result of actual or
threatened violence to her or her children is not regarded as
intentionally homeless and may qualify for full and permanent rehousing if they have a priority need, or for lesser
assistance.

The Matrimonial Homes Act 1983 gives the High Court or
county court power to make orders relating to the rights of
occupation of all spouses. If one spouse has a right of occupation under section 1(1) of the Act, the court may make an
order:

(a) declaring, enforcing or restricting the exercise of that
     right;
(b) prohibiting, suspending or restricting the exercise by
     either spouse of the right to occupy the home;
(c) requiring either spouse to permit the other to exercise
     that right.

Orders under the Act may relate to only part of the
premises; require the party in occupation to pay, for instance,
repairs and rent or mortgage repayments; and be for a limited
period of time, or an interim order pending divorce or the
finding of alternative accommodation.

Under the Domestic Violence and Matrimonial Proceedings Act 1976, the county court has power to grant injunctions
to either spouses or cohabitees which may exclude the other
party from the whole or part of the matrimonial home; or
require the other party to permit the applicant to enter and

remain in the whole or part of the matrimonial home. This Act is of particular importance to cohabitees who are not protected under the Matrimonial Homes Act 1983. In the case of *Davis* v. *Johnson* [1979], it was held that a joint tenant could be excluded from premises in favour of his partner.

Spouses may seek remedies under section 16 of the Domestic Proceedings and Magistrates' Courts Act 1978, which provides that on proof of use, or threatened use, of violence a magistrates' family proceedings court may make an order requiring a respondent spouse to leave the matrimonial home. It may also make an order requiring the occupant to permit the applicant to enter and remain.

The availability of remedy to non-spouses rests in resort being made more often to the county court jurisdiction under the 1976 Act than to the family proceedings court. Exclusion of either party from a joint home is a draconian power. The Court of Appeal has given guidance on criteria for the making and length of ouster orders:

(a) *Children's needs*   The welfare of children will be one and often an important factor but is not 'the first and paramount' criterion (*Richards* v. *Richards* [1984]).
(b) *The conduct of the parties*   This must be such as to justify refusal of one to live with the other. Violence would be a justification, tension or mere dislike would probably not (*Richards* v. *Richards* [1984]).
(c) *Parties' needs and resources*   Particularly the ability to find other accommodation including the strength and likely success of claims for re-housing by the housing authority.
(d) *Other considerations*   These include the possibility of a reconciliation; the length of time the parties have lived apart; the imminence of matrimonial proceedings.

Proceedings under the 1976 and 1978 Acts are only intended to provide short-term remedies; 3 months should normally be the limit (Practice Direction 1978).

Personal protection
Criminal proceedings are rarely brought in cases of domestic violence, although they have increased following implementation of the Police and Criminal Evidence Act 1984, which

makes one spouse a compellable witness against another unless they are jointly charged. Compensation can now be obtained from the Criminal Injuries Compensation Board in such cases but the success of applications is dependent on satisfying strict qualifying conditions (HMSO, 1986).

Rather than prosecution of the perpetrator or compensation for injury, the need is usually for protection for the victim and other members of the family. This may be obtained by *judicial separation* on the basis of one of the 'five facts' on which divorce petitions are founded but without the need to establish irretrievable breakdown, or by means of an injunction. A decree of judicial separation relieves the petitioner from the duty of cohabiting with the respondent and orders may be made regarding the custody and welfare of children and financial relief.

Injunctions

Where any non-molestation orders, matrimonial or other related proceedings are pending in the High Court or county court, an injunction may be sought restraining one spouse, usually the husband, from molesting, assaulting or otherwise interfering with the wife and children. The county court has power under the Domestic Violence and Matrimonial Proceedings Act 1976 to grant an injunction on the application of either party to a marriage or a cohabitee, whether or not they are seeking other relief. The injunction may restrain the respondent from molesting the applicant or a child living with the applicant, and exclude him from the home or compel him to admit the applicant to the home. Molestation includes all forms of physical interference and pestering, following about, abusive letters and phone calls, etc. Although all children under age 18 come within the definition, it is doubtful whether an adult son or daughter being molested by the defendant would be protected under the Act (Bromley and Lowe, 1987, p. 162).

An injunction is a powerful order non-compliance with which amounts to contempt of court and puts the party in default at risk of imprisonment. Injunctions are only used by the courts as a last resort. Where danger of serious injury or irreparable damage is real and immediate, an injunction may be granted *ex parte*.

An applicant who has been forced to leave the matrimonial

home before taking legal action can apply, provided the violence took place while the parties were living together. The more recent the incident, the more likely the relief (*McClean* v. *Nugent* [1979], and *O'Neill* v. *Williams* [1984]). In the High Court injunctions containing any of the above provisions may be sought independently of other proceedings (Supreme Court Act 1981, s.37, RSC Order 90).

Power of arrest

Committing a party in default to prison requires their apprehension and presence before the court. This may take some time to achieve and leave a spouse or partner in danger of attack. To avoid this, section 2 of the 1976 Act provides that a power of arrest may be attached whenever injunctions are granted restraining the defendant from using violence against the applicant, or a child living with the applicant, or excluding him from the matrimonial home or the area surrounding it. The power can be attached only if the person has in the past caused actual bodily harm to the applicant or child concerned and the court considers it likely to happen again. The circumstances in which a power of arrest may be attached are even more limited than those in which injunctions may be granted and should normally be limited to 3 months' duration (Practice Notice 1981).

Where there is a power of arrest, any constable may arrest the defendant if there is reasonable cause for suspecting that he is in breach of an injunction. Once arrested, the defendant must be brought before a judge within 24 hours (excluding Sundays, Christmas Day and Good Friday), and may not be released within that time except on a judge's direction.

In the magistrates' family proceedings court the remedies available depend on the level of risk. If the respondent has already used or threatened to use violence against the applicant or any child of the family, a family proceedings court may make an order that the other spouse shall not use or threaten violence or incite anyone else to do so. However, where there is either substantial evidence of the respondent causing physical injury to the applicant or a child of the family or evidence of a threat to do so and actual violence against another person, or the respondent has threatened to use violence in breach of a previous order, the court may exclude a spouse from the matrimonial home or order that the applicant be permitted to return. The order forbids the respondent to use violence or to enter the matrimonial home (1978 Act, s.16).

In addition, if the court is satisfied that the respondent has already physically injured the applicant or a child of the family, and that it is essential for the efficacy of the order, the magistrates may attach a power of arrest to the order. This will have the same effect as under the 1976 Act. If no power of arrest is attached, an applicant may apply for the arrest of a respondent in breach of a personal protection order.

6 Local authorities' powers and duties

Services for children in need

The presumption under the Act is that social work intervention, when needed, will wherever possible be in the form of the provision of supportive services to children and their families on a partnership basis. Part III can be seen as the cornerstone of the Act so far as child care work is concerned. Under section 17 local authorities have a positive duty to:

> safeguard and promote the welfare of children within their area who are in need; and so far is consistent with that duty promote the upbringing of such children by their families, by providing a range and level of services appropriate to those children's needs.

A child 'in need' is defined under Section 17(10) as one who is unlikely 'to achieve or maintain, or to have the opportunity of achieving or maintaining, a reasonable standard of health or development without the provision to him of services by a local authority. . .', or his health or development is likely to be significantly impaired, or further impaired, without the provision of such services; or he is disabled. 'Development' means physical, intellectual, emotional, social or behavioural development, and 'health' means physical or mental health (s. 17(11)). Local authorities also have preventative and investigative duties under the Act which relate to all children. These include the duty to 'take reasonable steps' through the provision of services detailed in Schedule 2, Part I, 'to prevent children within their area suffering ill-treatment or neglect'; (para 4), and to 'take reasonable steps' designed to reduce the need to bring care, criminal or other family proceedings relating to them (Allen, 1990).

The whole range of services which local authorities must or may provide in order to carry out their preventative role are set out in Part III and schedule 2 part I (DoH (1991a) Vol. 2). These include:

1. *Day care*   Local authorities are under a duty to provide such day care for children in need within their area who are aged five or under and not yet attending schools, 'as is appropriate' (s. 18), and may provide day care for other children of the same age even if they are not in need. The Nursery and Child Minders Regulation Act 1948 and all its regulations are repealed and replaced by Part 10 and Schedule 9 of the Children Act 1989 and new regulations (DoH (1991a) Vol. 2). Local authorities are under a duty to review both their provision of day care, and that provided by others required to register under the Act, and by child minders, for children under eight years. In addition to providing day care local authorities have a duty under the Act, together with the local education authority, to review provision of day care and the availability of child minders, for children under the age of eight, on a three yearly basis.

2. *Accommodation*   Local authorities are under a duty to provide accommodation for any child in need within their area who appear to them to require it (s.20). The provision of accommodation, which replaces reception into care under the Child Care Act 1980 section 2, is a voluntary arrangement; the child's wishes and feelings must be ascertained and 'given due consideration'. Anyone with parental responsibility (see p. 47) may prevent the placement of the child in accommodation or remove the child from accommodation at any time (s.20 (7) and (8)). Children in need who have reached the age of sixteen whose welfare the authority consider likely to be seriously prejudiced if accommodation is not provided must also be provided with accommodation regardless of the wishes of anyone with parental responsibility. Children in accommodation, together with those who are in care (see below p. 72), or on remand, come within the category of being 'looked after' by the local authority. There are both general

duties and detailed regulations in regard to all children who are 'looked after' (DoH (1991a) Vols 3 and 4 and Allen, 1990).

3. *Aftercare* The margin heading for section 24 of the Children Act 'Advice and assistance for certain children' reflects a real difficulty with terminology now that only children who are the subject of care orders can be referred to as being in care, whereas the duties and powers in section 24 apply to all children who have been looked after by the local authority, including those who have been accommodated in health service or voluntary provision, after reaching the age of 16 and who are still under 21. The Act provides that all those in the above category, who appear to be in need and ask for help, must be advised and befriended and where necessary given assistance in kind or in exceptional circumstances in cash.

A very helpful report which examines the legal, policy and practice implications of making proper provision for youngsters reaching adulthood without family support is available from the pressure group First Key (Stein, 1991). The author of this report was also involved in the preparation of the good practice guidance from the Department of Health (DoH (1991a) Vol. 3 Chapter 9).

4. *Services for families* Schedule 2 Part I sets out the range of services which local authorities are under either a duty or have power to provide. The mandatory provisions include: the identification of children in need and the provision of information about available services; the maintenance of a register of disabled children and the provision of services for disabled children which enable them to lead as normal lives as possible; the prevention of abuse and neglect and the committing of crimes by children; provision to reduce the need to bring care or criminal proceedings; the provision of services for children living with their families including family centres and to enable children living apart from their families to live with them. There is also a duty when considering day or foster care to consider the different racial groups represented in the area. The services which local authorities are empowered to provide include assistance to enable a suspected abuser to leave the home in order to allow a child to remain.

7 Children in need of protection

The duty to investigate

Department of Health guidance on inter-agency cooperation in child protection work, *Working Together* (DoH, 1991b) emphasizes the difficulty of striking the right balance between avoiding unnecessary intrusion in families whilst protecting children at risk from significant harm. The provisions in Part V of the Act relate to the powers to intervene and statutory controls on those powers. They should, however, always be read within the central philosophy of the Act that court intervention is a last resort, only to be pursued if voluntary arrangements have failed or are clearly inappropriate (Moore, 1992).

Local authorities may be put under a duty to make investigations into a child's circumstances either when there is information which gives 'reasonable grounds to suspect that a child who lives, or is found, in their area is suffering or is likely to suffer significant harm' (s.47) or they are informed of the making of an emergency protection order, or the placing of a child in police protection. The duty may also arise as a result of a court direction to investigate (s.37) (DoH, 1991a).

When put under a duty to investigate local authorities have to take all reasonable steps to ensure that access to the child is obtained and refusal of access or information about the child's whereabouts constitutes grounds for obtaining an emergency protection order, and a duty to do so unless workers are 'satisfied that his welfare can be satisfactorily safeguarded' in some other way. Similarly refusal to cooperate with an assessment of 'the state of the child's health or development or of the way in which he has been treated' in order to determine 'whether or not the child is suffering, or is likely to suffer, significant harm' may lead to an application for a child assessment order under s.43.

Court ordered investigations

Under previous legislation a court could make care or supervision orders on its own initiative, or on application by a local authority, in 'exceptional circumstances' in the interests of the child's welfare, in various proceedings in which decisions regarding children were being made. This effectively provided a 'back door' into care without the need to establish statutory grounds, and was strongly criticized by the Law Commission for this reason (Law Commission, 1987a). Under the 1989 Act care and supervision orders can only be made on the application of the local authority (or an authorized person) on the basis of satisfaction of the threshold conditions set out in s.31 (see below p. 70).

Where a court becomes sufficiently concerned about children, who are the subject of any other family proceedings, to consider the need for care or supervision they may order the local authority to investigate the child's circumstances (s.37) and consider whether to apply for a care or supervision order, provide services or assistance for the child or the family, or take any other action. When a court orders an investigation under section 37, provided there is reasonable cause to believe that the threshold conditions in section 31 are satisfied (s.38), it may at the same time make an interim care or supervision order. The local authority must report back within eight weeks and inform the court of any action they propose to take, or give reasons for a decision to take no action.

Compulsory intervention

The shift towards the use of voluntary arrangements rather than compulsory intervention is at the heart of the Children Act 1989. There will, however, always be cases in which cooperation is either not forthcoming or insufficient for the protection of the child and compulsory measures will be required. Previous legislation concerning local authorities' duties to investigate situations in which children appeared to be in need of protection contained an implicit presumption in favour of compulsory measures; under the Children Act the duty to investigate is strengthened and extended but the choice of route chosen to safeguard the child's welfare is left more open (Moore, 1992).

Guardians ad litem

To help maintain the focus on the child's welfare, in most public law proceedings a guardian *ad litem* (GAL), an independent social worker appointed by the court from a panel of Guardians *ad Litem* and Reporting Officers administered by the local authority, will be appointed, to safeguard the interests of the child, at an early stage. The role of the GAL which is considerably extended under the Act, is, as far as is possible, to ascertain the child's wishes and feelings, instruct the child's solicitor, advise the court on parties, the timetable for the proceedings, the making of interim orders, including possible discharge of an emergency protection order, and to prepare a report for the court. The details of the appointment, powers and duties of GALs are set out in the court rules (Family Proceedings Courts (Children Act) Rules 1991, rules 10 and 11) and guidance (DoH (1991a) Vol. 7). Where the child and the GAL disagree over the child's needs, a child of sufficient age and understanding may give his own instructions to his solicitor, and the GAL will represent her own views to the court, with legal representation where necessary.

The protection of children in an emergency

The immediate protection of children in any kind of emergency can only be achieved by the provision of wide powers available without delay, either to ensure that a child is removed from a situation of danger, or remains in one of safety when threatened with removal. Preventing abuse of such powers requires that they shall only be exercisable in circumstances in which immediate protection for the child cannot be secured in any other way, last for the minimum necessary time, and be open to challenge at the earliest opportunity. The contrasting dissatisfactions with place of safety orders under the Children and Young Persons Act 1969, informed the provisions in Part V of the Children Act (Blom-Cooper, 1987; Butler-Sloss, 1988; Allen, 1990; Ball 1989). The extent to which the former imprecise and broadly framed provisions allowed discrepant and sometimes abusive practice explains the detail contained in Part V, which leaves little margin for discretionary interpretation.

Emergency protection orders

The Emergency Protection Order is intended for use only in real emergencies: anyone may apply to a court, or, with leave of the justices' clerk, to a single justice who is member of the family proceedings panel, *ex parte* (without anyone who might oppose the application either being present or being served notice) for an order, on the grounds that

> 'there is reasonable cause to believe that the child is likely to suffer insignificant harm if ... he is not removed to accommodation provided by or on behalf of the applicant; or ... he does not remain in the place in which he is then being accommodated', or where enquiries are being made by a local authority, anyone authorised by them, or by the NSPCC, and they are denied access to the child (s.44).

An EPO may be made for up to eight days and the child or anyone with parental responsibility may apply to a court for discharge of the order after 72 hours, provided they were not served notice and were not present when the order was made. An EPO may be extended once for up to seven days if the court has reasonable cause to believe that the child will suffer significant harm if it is not extended. During the period that an EPO is in force the local authority will have limited parental responsibility and will therefore be able to make day to day decisions in regard to the child, whilst parents retain their parental responsibility subject to the EPO. There is a presumption of reasonable contact between parents and child, however the court may lay down requirements regarding the contact which shall or shall not take place, and concerning more than routine medical treatment or investigation – which a child old enough to decide may refuse (DoH (1991a) Vol. 1, *Gillick* v. *West Norfolk Health Authority* [1986], although it now looks possible that refusal may be over-ridden by a person with parental responsibility or a court (in *re R*. [1991], Lawson, 1991).

Police powers
Police protection
Under section 46 where a constable has reasonable cause to believe that a child would otherwise be likely to suffer significant harm he may remove the child to suitable accommodation or take reasonable steps to ensure that he remains where he is. The section sets out in great detail the steps that must be taken by the constable to ensure that parents, the local authority and the designated police officer responsible for inquiring into the case are informed, and that the child's wishes and feelings are considered. Police protection may only last for up to 72 hours, however during that time the designated officer may apply for an emergency protection order under section 44. If granted this will begin with the first day on which the child was taken into police protection.

Police warrants
Where it is either apparent at the time of the application for an EPO, or subsequently, that anyone attempting to exercise power under the order is being, or is likely to be, denied entry to premises or access to the child, a court or single justice may issue a warrant authorizing a police constable to exercise those powers using force if necessary (s.48(9)).

Entry of premises to save life and limb
The Police and Criminal Evidence Act 1984 (s.17(1)) restates the common law power of the police to enter and search any premises for the purposes of 'saving life or limb'. Where appropriate, exercise of this power could be followed by reception of the child into police protection.

Recovery order
Where a child in care or the subject of an emergency protection order or in police protection has been removed or run away from care, or is being kept away from any person who has care of them as a result of that order, the court may issue a recovery order under section 50. The order operates as a direction to produce the child, and authorizes their removal by any authorized person, and the entry and search of specified premises by a police constable. Taking or keeping a child in these circumstances constitutes an offence (s.49) unless the premises at which the child is being kept is a voluntary home,

registered children's home or foster home issued with a certificate as a refuge under section 51 of the Act (The Refuges (Children's Homes and Foster Placements) Regulations 1991 and DoH (1991a) Vol. 4).

Child assessment order

This is a new order which had no parallel in previous legislation. It may be applied for only in court, on notice, by a local authority or the NSPCC (as 'authorized person') on the grounds that there is reasonable cause to believe that the child is suffering or is likely to suffer, significant harm; that an assessment of the child's health and development are necessary, and that it is unlikely that a satisfactory assessment will be made in the absence of an order. If the court hearing the application believes that an EPO is justified then it should make one instead of the order applied for. Guidance suggests that CAOs will only be appropriate in cases in which 'a decisive step to obtain an assessment is needed ... and informal arrangements to have such an assessment carried out have failed.' (DoH (1991a) Vol. I para 4.8).

8   Care and supervision

Care proceedings

The only means whereby a local authority can assume parental responsibility in regard to a child under the age of seventeen, or sixteen if married (other than for the very short term of remand or an EPO) is by means of a care order made by a court, on the basis that the threshold conditions are satisfied, and that the order is likely to contribute positively to the child's welfare (s.1(5)). Under section 31(2):

> A court may only make a care order or a supervision order if it is satisfied –
> (a)   that the child concerned is suffering, or is likely to suffer, significant harm; and
> (b)   that the harm, or likelihood of harm, is attributable to –
> (i)   the care given to the child, or likely to be given to him if the order were not made, not being what it would be reasonable to expect a parent to give him; or
> (ii)   the child being beyond parental control.

Under the Act 'harm' is defined as ill-treatment or the impairment of health or development (further defined in s.31(9)); and whether harm suffered is significant depends on comparison with 'that which could reasonably be expected of a similar child'. It would seem inevitable that in due course a body of case law will refine these definitions.

Proceedings under section 31 and most other applications

for public law orders are commenced in a magistrates' court, unless they result from an investigation ordered under section 37 in which case they are heard by the court ordering the investigation. Cases commenced in the magistrates' court may be transferred, either laterally to another family proceedings court able to hear the application more quickly, or, on the basis of statutory criteria, to the local county court care centre. Exceptionally cases will be referred on from the care centre to the Family Division of the High Court. The diagram (Figure 1) shows the court and appeal structure for family proceedings (Eckelaar and Dingwall (1990) Ch.7).

Prior to a final hearing an interim care order or supervision order, or any private law orders under section 8 of the Act may be made on the basis that there are reasonable grounds to believe that the threshold conditions exist. The presumption that delay is harmful, and the provision within the court rules for directions hearings and the establishment of timetables for proceedings, means that any interim order beyond the first, which may be for up to eight weeks, will have to be well justified.

Procedure and orders
Directions hearings, the setting of timetables for the proceedings, may be dealt with by a justices' clerk. All reports and witnesses statements will have been exchanged before the hearing which will result in magistrates having to read and assimilate a considerable volume of paperwork before the hearing. Courts, including the magistrates' family proceedings courts have to give reasons for their decisions, and all parties have a right of appeal (Figure 1). Although the proceedings are single stage civil proceedings courts have to be satisfied that the threshold criteria set out in section 31(2) are satisfied before they decide which, if any (s.(45)), order to make. The orders available are:

(a) a care order;
(b) a supervision order to the local authority or in certain circumstances to a probation officer. The order may include directions to the child; a residence requirement; impose requirements on a person responsible for the child (with consent); or require the child to attend for medical examinations, or, if the relevant conditions are

met, to undergo psychiatric or medical treatment. Supervision orders cease to have effect after one year unless extended by a court up to a maximum of three years (s.35 and Schedule 3 Parts I and II).

(c)   Any section 8 order;

(d)   A family assistance order under section 16.

As in all proceedings under the Act the court has to be satisfied, before making any order, that making the order 'would be better for the child than making no order at all' (s.1(5)).

The effect of a care order

The effect of a care order, which lasts until the child is eighteen, unless discharged, is to give the local authority parental responsibility for the child together with the parents, who retain the right to exercise any aspects of their parental responsibility which is not in conflict with local authority decisions in respect of the child's upbringing. Children in care, together with those in accommodation under the Act or other legislation, come under local authorities' duty to children looked after by them. Regulations regarding the placements of all children 'looked after' by the local authority, which includes those in accommodation as well as in care, are detailed and elaborated on in Volume 3 of the Department of Health's Guidance (DoH (1991a)) and in the Placement of Children (General) Regulations 1991 and the Placement of Children with Parents Etc. Regulations 1991.

Secure accommodation

The use of 'accommodation provided for the purposes of restricting liberty' by local authorities for children whom they are looking after is subject to restriction, both in terms of the circumstances in which children may be locked up, and the maximum periods for which this may last. Liberty may only be restricted if the following criteria are satisfied:

s.25(1):
(a)   that –
  (i)   he has a history of absconding and is likely to abscond from any other description of accommodation; and
  (ii)   if he absconds he is likely to suffer significant harm; or
(b)   that if he is kept in any other description of accommodation he is likely to injure himself or any other persons.

If the above criteria are satisfied a child may be kept in secure accommodation for up to 72 hours without a court order. Children under the age of 13 may only be placed in secure accommodation with the direct authority of the Secretary of State. If the local authority propose to restrict liberty for more than 72 hours or an aggregate of 72 hours in a 28-day period they must obtain a court order. The restrictions on the use of secure accommodation do not apply to children subject to detention under mental health legislation, but they do apply to all children accommodated by health or local education authorities or in residential care, nursing or mental nursing homes. Children in voluntary children's homes and registered children's homes may not be kept in secure accommodation (DoH (1991a) Vol. 1 and Vol. 7). Anyone with parental responsibility may remove a child in accommodation whose liberty is being restricted at any time (s.20(8)).

Applications for secure accommodation orders for children in care or in accommodation, apart from those who are remanded into accommodation as a result of committing criminal offences, are made to the family proceedings court (or the county or High Court). If granted the order may be for three months in the first instance and may be renewed on application to the court for periods of up to six months. Applications in regard to children on remand are to the youth or other magistrates' court, and last for the period of the remand up to a maximum of 28 days.

In all secure accommodation proceedings the child must be legally represented, or have refused such representation. In non-criminal proceedings applications to keep children in secure accommodation are proceedings to which section 1 of the Act (see p.51) apply, and in which a guardian *ad litem* must be appointed unless the court is satisfied that it is not necessary in the interests of the child.

Contact between children in care, parents and certain other people

The law regarding parental contact with children in care is profoundly altered by section 34 of the Children Act which specifically makes provision for contact with children in care for whom section 8 contact orders are not available. Local authorities have a duty to promote contact between a child in care and his/her parents and certain other people specified in the section, unless directed otherwise by court order. Courts must consider contact arrangements, which should generally be able to be agreed between the parties but may need to be specified, before making a care order. Parents and others may challenge local authorities' variation of agreed levels of contact, and if an authority wishes to deny contact to anyone entitled to it under the Act a court order must be obtained (s.34(4)).

Supervision

Supervision orders under the Children Act 1989 section 35 and schedule 3 part I, like care orders, may only be made if the threshold conditions in section 31 and the principles in section 1 are satisfied. A supervision order puts the child under the supervision of a designated local authority or probation officer for up to one year. The order may be discharged by a court at an earlier date, or extended for up to a maximum of three years. The order may contain directions that the child reside in a particular place, or complies with directions given by the superviser to participate in particular activities for up to a maximum of 90 days. Schedule 3 paras 4 and 5 give detailed directions regarding the consents that have to be given and the criteria for including requirements as to medical or psychiatric treatment under a supervision order (DoH(1991a) Vol. 1).

Interim supervision orders may be made prior to final determination of a case. There is also a new order under the Act to include requirements for up to 90 days in relation to a responsible person, defined as any person with parental responsibility or any other person with whom the child is living. These requirements include taking reasonable steps to ensure that the child complies with directions given by the superviser, or ensuring that the child complies with requirements to participate in activities or receive treatment (Schedule 3 para 3). (Allen (1990) Ch. 11).

9   Adoption, residence orders and wardship

When children in local authority care are unable to be rehabilitated with their own parents or relatives, efforts will be made to ensure that they grow up in a permanent substitute family. For some, this will mean severance of all legal ties with their birth family and complete legal assimilation, through adoption, into a new one. For a few children, the less final, though potentially less secure route, may be through a residence order.

Wardship comes at the end of the section on child care law because ultimately the jurisdiction can, even after limitations on its use by local authorities (Children Act 1989 s.100), provide a safety net when all statutory provision fails to safeguard the welfare of the child.

Adoption
Adoption was first introduced into English law in 1926 with the objective of providing permanent and secure care in a family for orphan children or those whose natural parents were permanently unable or unwilling to bring them up. Under the Adoption of Children Act 1926 and all subsequent legislation, an adoption order effects a complete and virtually irrevocable legal transfer of a child from one family to another. While a detailed consideration of adoption law is beyond the scope of this book and those working in the field will need to make reference to a specialist work (Cretney and Masson, 1990), the legal issues surrounding adoption feature in many areas of child care practice. Apart

from the introduction of the Adoption Contact Register adoption law has not been substantially altered by the Children Act 1989. It is, at the time of writing, the subject of a major inter-departmental review and new legislation is likely within the next few years (DoH (1991a) Vol. 9).

Local authority social workers may be involved in adoption proceedings specifically because adoption may be being considered for children on their caseload or because they may have to prepare the very detailed report required by the court in all adoption cases under Schedule 2 of the Adoption Rules 1984. There is a sense in which all social workers are adoption workers since the Adoption Act 1976 places on all local authorities a statutory duty to:

> establish and maintain within their area a service designed to meet the needs in relation to adoption, of:
>
> (a)   children who have been or may be adopted,
> (b)   parents and guardians of such children, and
> (c)   persons who have adopted or may adopt a child, and for that purpose to provide the requisite facilities, or secure that they are provided by approved adoption societies. (s.1(1)).

The fact that the making of an adoption order effects such a profound change in a child's legal status is mirrored in the strict requirements laid down for all stages of the adoption process. An adoption order can – even if all the parties are agreeing – only be made by an authorized court, that is in the magistrates' family proceedings court, the county court or, in certain circumstances, the High Court. Currently the statutory provisions and procedural rules are to be found in the Adoption Act 1976, Adoption Rules 1984, the Adoption Agency Regulations 1983, and the Adoption (Amendment) Rules 1991.

In order to ensure the 'normality' of the new family and that the child's welfare is the first consideration, the law provides strict requirements as to who may adopt or place for adoption, how the process is conducted, the consent or dispensing with the consent of the natural parents and how the interests of the child are both assessed by the agency and put before the court. An independent checking mechanism by the appointment of an independent reporting officer for the parents or where necessary a guardian ad litem to safeguard the welfare of the child is built into the system, to ensure that all the legal requirements have been met and that the order is in the child's interests.

At the heart of all the statutory provisions, but not overriding any of the procedural rules, is the requirement that:

> the court or adoption agency shall have regard to all the circumstances, the first consideration being given to the need to safeguard and promote the welfare of the child throughout his childhood; and shall so far as is practicable ascertain the wishes and feelings of the child regarding the decision and give due consideration to them, having regard to his age and understanding. (Adoption Act 1976, s.6)

Safeguarding the child's welfare may be better achieved by means of other orders which make a less drastic alteration in his legal status than that effected by adoption. Under the Children Act 1989 in any family proceedings the court may make orders other than those applied for, for instance a residence order (see p. 52) instead of an adoption order.

Freeing for adoption

An adoption order is made, provided all the formalities are in order and the court decides that the making of the order is in the child's interests, following an application by the prospective adopters; the natural parents will have given their consent, or that consent will have been dispensed with by the court on one of the grounds set out in section 16 of the Act.

In cases in which either the child is already in the care of the agency and the issue of parental consent is in doubt, or where the mother wants the child adopted before any specific application is ready, the agency may apply to the court for an order freeing the child for adoption (s.18). The effect of the order, to which the parents must consent, or their consent be dispensed with, is to extinguish existing parental responsibility and vest it in the agency which will hold it until an adoption order is made. Natural parents will be informed if an order has been made or the child placed for adoption after a year, unless they sign a declaration that they do not wish to be further involved. If they have not signed the declaration and the child has not been placed, they may apply for revocation of the freeing order. Despite the considerable and desirable changes in adoption law that have been introduced since 1926 – mostly designed to equate the position of adopted children with natural children as regards legitimacy and inheritance, or as with the provisions introduced in the Children Act 1975, to discourage the somewhat artificial family structure resulting from adoption by step-parents – there is current concern over the extent to which legal provisions first conceived when almost all the children placed for adoption were illegitimate white babies, and most adopters childless couples, provide adequately for the very changed situation where increasingly the children are older and often coming to adoption with complex packages of previous relationships (Ball, 1987; Hoggett, 1987; Thoburn, 1991).

Residence

Residence orders under section 8 of the Children Act 1989 replace custodianship as the means of providing security short of adoption for carers and children. Although custodianship orders were not widely used during the relatively few years (1985–1991) during which they were available, they added flexibility to the long-term provision that could be made for children who needed security in their placement, but for whom the complete severance from their birth family was not appropriate (Thoburn, 1988). They proved particularly useful to relatives and others who had looked after a child, who was not an orphan, for many years on an informal basis, and who, owing to a lacuna or gap in the law, had no recourse other than wardship if a parent sought to reclaim the child. After implementation of the custodianship provisions in 1985 in the Children Act 1975, even without the consent of the child's parents, carers with whom the child had lived for three years could apply for custodianship, and the issue would be decided on the basis of the child's interests being paramount. The applicants for custodianship orders had an added safeguard which has disappeared under the Children Act, that when an application was pending no one could remove the child without leave of the court.

Residence orders may be made by courts hearing adoption applications whether or not the parents have agreed to adoption. The order gives the person(s) in whose favour the order is made parental responsibility (see p. 47) for the duration of the order as well as determining 'with whom the child is to live' (s.8(1)) and may have any conditions the court considers necessary attached. Residence orders differ from adoption in that they generally come to an end when the child is sixteen, though need not do so if the court considers the case exceptional (s.9(6)); the child's name may only be changed with the consent of all those with parental responsibility, or the court's direction; and, carers with a residence order cannot appoint a guardian for the child in the event of their death, or consent to the child's adoption.

Wardship

Wardship is a common law rather than a statutory jurisdiction; however, procedure in wardship cases is governed by the Supreme Court Act 1981 and the Rules of the Supreme Court (Order 90, rules 3–11). Under these rules, anyone with a declared personal or professional interest can make the child a ward of court by taking out an originating summons which has the immediate effect that, from that moment, no important step, such as leaving the country or moving residence or school or getting married or undergoing major surgery, may be taken without leave of the court. Unless an appointment for a hearing is made within 21 days, wardship lapses. If an appointment is made, the child continues to be a ward until the full hearing unless there is a successful interim application to de-ward (1981 Act, s.41).

The High Court has exclusive jurisdiction to make a child a ward and to de-ward, but all intermediate decisions may now be transferred to and from the county court in accordance with a practice direction (1986) of the President of the Family Division.

'A ward of court is a child whose guardian is the High Court' (Law Commission, 1987b); the effect of this is that whoever has day-to-day care and control of a ward, no important decision may be taken in his/her life without reference to the court; and the judge has the power to make infinitely flexible arrangements within the constraints of the criteria that all decisions have to recognize that the welfare of the child is paramount.

The power of the High Court to assume guardianship of minors in need of protection, now primarily concerned with the welfare of children, stems from the ancient doctrine of *parens patriae* – the king as father of his people. It is a measure of the increasing part that wardship was playing in the field of child care law that the jurisdiction was subjected to critical

Table 2 *The incidence of originating summons in wardship (principal and district registries)*

Year	Principal registry	District registry	Total
1971	622	n.a.	622
1981	822	1,081	1,903
1982	875	1,426	2,301
1983	802	1,338	2,140
1984	952	1,456	2,408
1985	965	1,850	2,815
1986	1,149	2,250	3,399
1990	1,146	3,575	4,721

Source: *Judicial Statistics*, 1990, Lord Chancellor's Department

scrutiny by the Law Commission as part of the family law review of child care law (see Law Commission, 1987b).

The growth of the use of wardship by local authorities was a recent phenomenon. Almost all of the considerable rise in the numbers of originating summons in the last two decades were accounted for by applications made by or with the agreement of local authorities, whose applications by 1990 made up more than 60 per cent of the total (Table 2).

The range and flexibility of orders available under the Children Act 1989 are intended to render use of wardship unnecessary in most cases, and it is no longer available to local authorities as a route by which to secure care or supervision orders (s.100). As a result the number of wardship cases is likely to drop dramatically from the high of the late 1980s. The jurisdiction still remains for private law proceedings and other issues relating to children in which there appears to be a lacuna in the law.

Before implementation of the Child Abduction Act 1984, making the child a ward of court was the only means of activating the 'stop list' whereby all ports and airports are alerted to prevent the removal of a child from the jurisdiction, and wardship may still be useful in cases which fall outside the provisions of that Act.

As a result of the much-publicized case of Jeanette, it is now established that any proposed sterilization of a mentally handicapped minor requires the authority of a judge in wardship and such a decision can only be taken on the basis of the individual welfare of the girl in question (*Re B. (A Minor) (Wardship: Sterilization)* [1987]). The issue of whether the High Court has an inherent jurisdiction to make similar decisions in respect of mentally handicapped adults is still unresolved, and is properly a matter for legislation.

The use of wardship to settle unresolved conflicts between those with parental responsibility for a child has been replaced by specific issue orders under the Children Act 1989 section 8.

PART III
THE LEGAL CONTEXT OF WORK WITH OTHER CLIENT GROUPS

10   Aspects of disability: mental disorder, the handicapped and elderly infirm

Mentally disordered people

A more detailed knowledge of mental health law is required by those appointed as approved social workers under the Mental Health Act 1983 than can be provided by a general text such as this and several specialist texts are available (Hoggett, 1990; Rashid and Ball, 1987; Gostin, Meacher and Olsen, 1983). In addition, an historical perspective such as that provided by Hoggett is necessary not only to appreciate the dramatic changes that have occurred this century in the statutory framework which determines the limits of intervention in the lives of mentally disordered people, but also to understand much of the present legislation. All local authority social workers, even if not authorized to exercise them, need to be aware of the statutory powers that exist in relation to the mentally ill and handicapped and the legal restraints that should prevent abuse of those powers.

The law relating to the treatment of mentally disordered patients in England and Wales is contained in the Mental Health Act 1983, which consolidated much of the 1959 Mental Health Act with substantial amendments introduced in the Mental Health (Amendment) Act 1982. Although the provisions of the 1983 Act differ substantially in detail from those of the 1959 Act, the principle on which treatment is provided – the innovative cornerstone of the earlier Act – has not altered:

Nothing in this Act shall be construed as preventing a patient who requires treatment for mental disorder from being admitted to any hospital or nursing home in pursuance of arrangements made in that behalf and without any application, order or direction rendering him liable to be detained under this Act or from remaining in any hospital or mental nursing home in pursuance of such arrangements after he has ceased to be so liable to be detained. (Mental Health Act 1983, s.131(1))

The powers to admit or detain mentally disordered people in hospital compulsorily can only be considered when all attempts to persuade the patient to accept treatment on a voluntary basis have failed, and then only in circumstances which meet the detailed requirements set out in the Act.

Definitions under the 1983 Act

The legislation refers 'to the reception, care and treatment of mentally disordered patients'. Under section 1(2), *mental disorder* means mental illness (which is not defined in the legislation), arrested or incomplete development of mind, psychopathic disorder and any other disorder or disability of mind.

Severe mental impairment means a state of arrested or incomplete development of mind which includes severe impairment of intelligence and social functioning and is associated with abnormally aggressive or seriously irresponsible conduct on the part of the person concerned.

Mental impairment means a state of arrested or incomplete development of mind (not amounting to severe mental impairment) which includes significant impairment of intelligence and social functioning and is associated with abnormally aggressive or seriously irresponsible conduct of the person concerned.

Psychopathic disorder means a persistent disorder or disability of mind, whether or not including significant impairment of intelligence, which results in abnormally aggressive or seriously irresponsible conduct on the part of the person concerned.

It is important to note that severe mental impairment, mental impairment and psychopathic disorder all require evidence of 'abnormally aggressive or seriously irresponsible conduct', and that behaviour due solely to promiscuity or immoral conduct, sexual deviancy, drugs or alcohol dependence is excluded from the definition of mental disorder (s.1(3)).

Approved social workers

The role and responsibilities of social workers working with the mentally ill were both enhanced and extended by the 1983 Act. As from October 1984, only approved social workers (ASWs) appointed and approved by their authorities 'as having appropriate competence in dealing with persons suffering from mental disorder' can carry out duties under the Act. The post-qualifying training requirement for ASWs involves a programme of at least 60 days' training (CCETSW, 1987).

The powers and duties of the ASW include interviewing patients in a suitable manner; making applications for admissions to hospital or helping nearest relatives to do so; applying to the county court to replace the nearest relative when that relative is preventing, on grounds the ASW considers unreasonable, the patient's removal to hospital (*W*. v. *L*. [1974]); conveying patients to hospital; entering and inspecting premises in which a mentally disordered person is living; and if necessary, applying for a warrant to search for and remove the patient (s. 135(1)) (see Hoggett, 1990; Rashid and Ball, 1987).

Nearest relatives

Relatives are defined under section 26 of the Mental Health Act 1983 with the 'nearest' higher on the list with the oldest in any category taking precedence regardless of sex:

- husband or wife;
- son or daughter;
- father or mother;
- brother or sister;
- grandparent;
- uncle or aunt;
- nephew or niece.

In practice, there are further extensions; for instance, a cohabitee may be regarded as a spouse after 6 months, and where there are no other relations, after five years a non-relative fellow lodger or landlady may be considered a relative for the purposes of the Act (Hoggett, 1990).

Compulsory powers

There are three procedures for applying for compulsory admission to hospital, without judicial proceedings, on the application of the nearest relative or an approved social worker supported by the recommendation of one or two doctors, and one – rarely used – for guardianship in the community. A patient already in hospital may become subject to compulsory detention on the basis of a report by the doctor in charge of his case, or in more extreme circumstances by a nurse. In addition, the police have the power to remove to a place of safety any person found in a public place who appears to be suffering from a mental disorder and to be in need of care or control, and an approved social worker (ASW) can apply for a warrant to authorize the police to enter premises to search for a mentally disordered person and, if necessary, remove them to a safe place.

The courts, or the Home Secretary, may make orders under the Act compulsorily detaining patients who have been accused of criminal offences. Each of these powers, or 'sections' as they are commonly known, need to be looked at separately.

Admission for assessment   Section 2 of the 1983 Act authorizes the detention of the patient for up to 28 days on an application by the nearest relative or someone authorized by them or by the county court to act on their behalf, or by an approved social worker, supported by recommendations from two doctors, one of whom must be an approved specialist in mental disorder and both of whom must have examined the patient either together or within 5 days of each other. The medical recommendation must be based on the fact that the patient

(a)   is suffering from mental disorder of a nature or degree which warrants the detention of the patient in a hospital for assessment (or for assessment followed by treatment) for at least a limited period; and

(b)   he ought to be so detained in the interests of his own safety or with a view to the protection of other persons.

The applicant is responsible for getting the patient to hospital, and may seek help from the ambulance service or the police. If patients escape, they may be apprehended and returned, but after 14 days from the date of the second medical recommendation authority to detail or admit the patient lapses. If patients reach the hospital within 14 days, authority to detain them lasts for 28 days unless steps are taken to detain for further treatment.

An order for discharge may be made in respect of a patient detained for assessment by the responsible medical officer, the managers or the nearest relative. If the patient applies to a Mental Health Review Tribunal within 14 days of admission to hospital, the tribunal may discharge the patient.

Admission for assessment in an emergency   In an emergency an application for assessment may be made with the support of only one doctor, who need not be a mental health specialist, though he should if possible have previous acquaintance with, and must have examined, the patient within the 24 hours prior to the patient's removal to hospital (s.4).

An emergency application, which authorizes detention for up to 72 hours, may be made either by the nearest relative or by an approved social worker. The application must not only state that it is 'of urgent necessity for the patient to be admitted and detained', but be supported by a statement from the recommending doctor indicating the length of the delay that would be caused by obtaining a second medical opinion, why this might result in harm and whether the harm would be caused to the patient or to those caring for the patient or to other people (Mental Health (Hospital Guardianship and Consent to Treatment) Regulations 1983, Form 7). After 72 hours, authority to detain the patient lapses, unless a second medical recommendation (made if the initial one was not) by a doctor 'approved as having special experience in the diagnosis or treatment of mental disorder' converts the emergency admission into a section 2 (28 days) admission.

Emergency procedures as introduced by the provisions of the Mental Health Act 1959 (s.29) were originally intended for exceptional use only. As with other similar provisions where the emergency procedure is either less complicated, or less demanding in terms of evidence, in practice the procedure intended for occasional emergency use became the normal route. This gave rise to considerable concern among those working with the mentally ill (Gostin, 1975, 1978; DHSS, 1976).

Under the 1983 Act, use of the procedure has been discouraged, in that the categories of person who make application for an emergency admission are restricted to nearest relatives and approved social workers. At the same time, stricter criteria for invoking the procedure were introduced and their observance encouraged by the regulations. It is a matter for continuing criticism, however, that patients can still be admitted under section 4 on a medical recommendation given by a doctor who may have no prior knowledge of the patient, nor any experience or expertise in the diagnosis of mental disorder (Hoggett, 1990, ch. 4).

Admission for treatment (s.3)   An application for admission for treatment under this section may be made by the nearest relative or, if the nearest relative objects, someone appointed by the county court to act as such or, with the agreement of the nearest relative, by an ASW. The applicant must have seen the patient within the previous 14 days and the application must be supported by recommendations by two doctors, one of them an approved specialist, to the effect that the patient

(a)   is suffering from mental illness, severe mental impairment, psychopathic disorder or mental impairment and his mental disorder is of a nature or degree which makes it appropriate for him to receive medical treatment in a hospital; and
(b)   in the case of a psychopathic disorder or mental impairment, such treatment is likely to alleviate or prevent a deterioration of his condition; and
(c)   it is necessary for the health and safety of the patient or for the protection of other persons that he should receive such treatment and it cannot be provided unless he is detained under this section.

The patient may then be detained, in the first instance, for up to 6 months, then for a further 6 months and thereafter for a year at a time on the basis of a report from the responsible medical officer (RMO) to the hospital managers which states that continued detention is necessary, using the same criteria as those justifying the initial admission.

Subject to certain safeguards, many forms of treatment except those which are irreversible may be administered to patients admitted or detained under section 3 without their consent, provided that a second medical opinion is sought (see also sections 57 and 58, and Hoggett, 1990).

While a patient is detained for treatment under section 3, discharge may be by the RMO, the managers or the nearest relative. If the RMO certifies that 'the patient if discharged would be likely to act in a manner dangerous to other persons or to himself' (s.25(d)), discharge by the nearest relative may be blocked. In those circumstances, the nearest relative can apply to a Mental Health Review Tribunal. The patient may also apply to be discharged by a Mental Health Review Tribunal within the first 6 months of detention and once during each subsequent period of renewal.

Patients already in hospital (s.5)   If it appears to the regis- tered medical practitioner in charge of the medical treatment of a voluntary in-patient that an application ought to be made for the patient's detention in hospital, he may provide the managers with a report in writing to that effect and the patient may be detained in hospital for 72 hours from the time the report was furnished. Under section 5(4), a nurse may, if no practitioner is available, furnish a report to the managers to record that fact in writing and the patient may be detained for up to 6 hours (s.5(4)).

Detention in a 'place of safety' (s.136)   A police officer find- ing a person who appears to be suffering from mental dis- order, and to be in need of care or control, in a public place may remove that person to a place of safety if he thinks it necessary in their interests or for the safety of others. The section authorizes detention for up to 72 hours for the purpose of medical and social work assessment, the patient most usually being detained in a police station or hospital. Use and possible abuse of the section have attracted attention from researchers and those concerned with the rights of the men- tally ill. Although the powers are not widely used outside London, there is evidence of considerable under-recording (Butler, 1975) and some pressure from MIND during the debate on the 1982 Amendment Act both to tighten the criteria and reduce the detention period to a maximum of 24 hours (Gostin, 1975).

Police warrant under s.135(1)   An ASW who has reason to believe that a mentally disordered person is not under proper care may apply to a magistrate for a warrant which will empower a police officer accompanied by an ASW and a doctor to enter premises, by force if necessary, and again, if it is considered necessary, to remove the mentally disordered person to a place of safety without formally 'sectioning' the person for up to 72 hours. There is no power to treat the patient without his/her consent under this procedure. Definitions under this section are difficult and there is some suspicion that its apparent very low rate of use masks considerable flouting of the law by the professionals involved (Hoggett, 1990).

Guardianship   When the 1959 Act was implemented, it was envisaged that compulsory care within the community would replace hospital orders for most patients. In fact only a minute number of guardianship orders were made. The 1983 Act provisions attempt to make guardianship more workable, though there is as yet little indication that many orders, either civil or criminal, are being made.

The rules as to the applicants and medical recommendations are similar to those for compulsory admission to hospital; the application is addressed to the local authority, and the proposed guardian may be an individual approved by the local authority who consents to act, or any social service authority which accepts responsibility. Under the 1983 Act, the guardian has the power to:

(i)   require the patient to reside at a place specified;
(ii)   attend at places and times specified for the purpose of medical treatment, occupation, etc.;
(iii)   require that access to the patient may be given to any doctor, ASW or other similar person.

Under the Act, patients may be transferred from hospital to guardianship and vice versa. The duration and termination of guardianship orders are very similar to those for patients admitted for treatment under section 3 (Rashid and Ball, 1987).

Orders made in criminal proceedings
Remands and interim orders under sections 35, 36 and 38 were introduced into the 1983 Act to provide for those cases in which a remand on bail with a condition of psychiatric assessment is considered impracticable, but the alternative of prison does not provide a suitable environment for such an assessment. This is an important issue for probation officers who may need to write social inquiry reports on mentally disordered offenders for whom use of these provisions may be appropriate (Stone, 1991a).

Remand to hospital for a report (s.35) Any person awaiting trial for an offence (except murder) punishable with imprisonment may, if the court is satisfied on medical evidence that there is reason to suggest that the accused is suffering from mental illness, psychopathic disorder, severe mental impairment (the four categories), may be remanded to a specified hospital with a bed available within 7 days for a 'report on his mental condition'. The remand may be for up to 28 days and is renewable for similar periods up to a total of 12 weeks. Offenders detained under this section cannot be compelled to accept treatment.

Remand of an accused person for treatment (s.36) Persons accused of offences punishable with imprisonment (excluding murder) who are certified by two registered medical practitioners to be suffering from 'mental illness or severe mental impairment of a nature or degree which makes it appropriate for them to be detained in hospital for treatment' may be remanded to hospital for treatment, which under this section cannot be refused.

Interim hospital orders (s.38) This section provides for a convicted offender to be made the subject of an interim hospital order on the evidence of two registered medical practitioners that the offender is suffering from one of the four categories of mental disorder and that 'there is reason to suppose that the disorder from which the defendant is suffering is such that it may be appropriate for a hospital order to be made in his case'.

This order authorizes admission to hospital within 28 days for an initial period of 12 weeks, which may be increased by periods of up to 28 days to a maximum of 6 months, provided that the offender's legal representative is heard if extensions are made.

Hospital or guardianship order (s.37)   A hospital order, which has the effect of an admission for treatment under section 3, may be made by a court sentencing for an imprisonable offence (except murder) on evidence of two registered medical practitioners of the existence of one of the four categories of mental disorder. If an order is made under section 37, the nearest relative does not have the power to discharge the patient, only to apply to the Mental Health Review Tribunal on the patient's behalf after 6 months; patients may make a similar application on their own behalf. The condition must be likely to respond to treatment or warrant guardianship, and the court must consider the order the most appropriate method of disposing of the case (for greater detail and a commentary, see Hoggett, 1990).

Restriction order (s.41)

> Where a hospital order is made in respect of an offender by the Crown Court and it appears to the court having regard to the nature of the offence, the antecedents of the offender, and the risk of his committing further offences if set at large that it is necessary for the protection of the public from serious harm so to do, the court may . . . order that the offender be subject to the special restriction set out in this section.

The restriction order can only be made in the Crown Court and has the effect of limiting the power to order discharge to the Secretary of State, who has to receive annual reports on the offender, or a Mental Health Review Tribunal. Discharge, when authorized, may be absolute or conditional (Rashid and Ball, 1987, ch. 4). Probation officers also need to be aware of the power that exists to allow the transfer of mentally disordered prisoners to hospital under sections 47 and 48 with possible restriction under section 49 (Stone, 1991a).

Mental Health Review Tribunals
Mental Health Review Tribunals provide an independent specialist forum before which almost all compulsorily detained patients can have their detention reviewed. There is a Tribunal

for each regional health authority and each panel has legal, medical and lay members 'who have such experience in administration, such knowledge of social services or such other qualifications and experience as the Lord Chancellor considers suitable'. A tribunal is made up of at least one member of each group with a lawyer presiding. Hoggett (1990) considers in detail the various applications that may be made to tribunals and the different procedures that apply.

The Court of Protection

Mentally disordered people, whether they are in hospital or not, may not be able to manage their own affairs and may be vulnerable to exploitation. If a mentally incapable person owns even a small amount of property, it is likely that the powers of the Court of Protection may have to be invoked. This court, which is an office of the Supreme Court, exists solely to deal with the affairs of people who are incapable of managing for themselves.

Proceedings in the Court of Protection are usually started by the patient's nearest relative by means of an originating application, but anyone can apply and social workers may find themselves needing to do so on behalf of a client. Before the court can intervene, it has to have a certificate from a registered medical practitioner that the patient is incapable by reason of medical disorder from conducting his own affairs, and either a simple certificate if the patient's income is under £1,000 and capital under £5,000 or, if larger amounts are involved, a sworn affidavit setting out particulars of property and affairs, details of relatives and the grounds for making the application.

The patient must be served with notice of the application or, if the matter is simple, the proposed summary order unless the court considers that the person is incapable of understanding. After that, the patient has at least 7 days or until the date of the hearing, whichever is later, in which to object in writing to the court. There is no provision for a patient to be heard in person.

The court can make any relative or anyone else who seems interested in the application a party to the proceedings, and any relative closer than the applicant should be informed. All this can take a considerable time; however, if there is urgent need for immediate protection, the court can make such interim orders as it considers necessary.

Once a patient is subject to the court's jurisdiction, it has exclusive control over all the person's property and affairs and wide powers to fulfil this function for the maintenance and benefit of the patient and family. Unless the patient's affairs are sufficiently straightforward to be dealt with by a simple order, the court will appoint a receiver, who will be empowered in very precise terms to protect the estate and use it for the patient's behalf and will have to render annual accounts. The receiver may be a relative, professional adviser or any other suitable person who is prepared to act. If there is no such individual, the Official Solicitor may be appointed.

The powers of the Court of Protection are massive and its procedures both cumbersome and expensive, in that not insubstantial fees deducted from the patient's property are charged. However, its powers provide protection from exploitation which cannot be achieved in any other way. The court's functions continue until the patient dies or, exceptionally, the court finds that it can discharge the receiver because patients have recovered sufficiently to manage their own affairs. Other less intrusive but correspondingly less effective measures which may be taken in regard to the affairs of mentally incapable people are usefully discussed in the context of legal rights (Cooper, 1990).

The physically handicapped and elderly infirm

Local authorities have a general power under section 29 of the National Assistance Act 1948 to make arrangements to promote the welfare of disabled people, to provide housing (Part III) and a duty under the Chronically Sick and Disabled Persons Act 1970 to inform themselves of the level of need within their area and to keep a register of disabled persons. Under the National Health Service and Community Care Act 1991, disabled persons or their carers may ask the local authority to assess a disabled person's needs for services and the local authority has to make a decision.

The main problem with all the legislation relating to disabled people is that it provides an enabling framework for good practice but that few provisions are mandatory. This is particularly the case with the 1970 Act, which has failed to live up to the high hopes of those responsible for its introduction.

Statutory provision to meet the particular needs of disabled persons are considered in outline by Rashid and Ball (1987) and in practical detail in the *Disability Rights Handbook* (Annual) and in regard to elderly people by Griffiths *et al.* (1990).

Compulsory removal from home

The compulsory removal from home of an elderly, infirm or chronically sick person who does not come within the terms of the Mental Health Act 1983, although it may occasionally be necessary in their interests, involves grave issues of civil liberties (Alison, 1980; Tinker, 1985; Cooper, 1990).

An order authorizing removal from home on these grounds can only be obtained from a court, or in an emergency *ex parte* from a single justice, if the statutory criteria are met. The power of removal under section 47(1) of the National Assistance Act 1948 applies only to persons who:

(a) are suffering from grave chronic disease or, being aged, infirm or physically incapacitated, are living in insanitary conditions, and

(b) are unable to devote to themselves, and are not receiving from other persons, proper care and attention.

The court procedure requires the Community Health Officer to certify in writing to the local authority that he is satisfied that an order is necessary. The local authority may apply to a magistrates' court for an order, which provided the court is satisfied that one is necessary, is limited to 3 months and extendable by another 3 months. The patient must be given 7 days' notice of the hearing and any hospital 7 days' notice of the arrival of the patient. The patient or anyone on their behalf may, having given 7 days' notice to the local authority, apply for discharge of the order after 6 weeks.

An emergency procedure, which as with admission for assessment under the Mental Health Act 1959 (s.29) has become the norm, was introduced by section 1 of the National Assistance (Amendment) Act 1951. Under this procedure, the local authority may make an *ex parte* application on the grounds set out in section 47(1) of the 1948 Act to a magistrates' court or single justice. The Community Health Officer and another registered medical practitioner, usually the patient's general practitioner, have to certify that in their opinion, 'it is necessary in the interests of that person to remove him without delay' (1951 Act, s.1(1)). Under this procedure, the initial period of detention is for 3 weeks (Griffiths *et al.*, 1990; Cooper, 1990).

When anyone is admitted to hospital under the above provisions or into accommodation provided under Part III of the 1948 Act, the local authority has a statutory responsibility to take reasonable steps to mitigate loss or damage, and under section 48(2) of the 1948 Act, has a power of entry to the previous place of residence in order to carry out this duty. Local authorities have detailed procedures to be followed by workers to ensure that their responsibilities under this section are met.

11 Young offenders and the youth court

Background

Special magistrates' courts for juvenile offenders were first set up under the Children Act 1908 to provide procedures more suitable for children and to protect juveniles from contact with, and contamination by, adult offenders. The law relating to criminal proceedings in the juvenile court is currently contained in the Children and Young Persons Acts of 1933 and 1969 as considerably amended, most recently by provisions in the Criminal Justice Act 1991 extending the jurisdiction to include 17-year-olds and changing the name to youth court.

From the beginning, courts for young offenders were also given jurisdiction over juveniles who were thought to be in need of care, thus starting the elision of welfare and justice which until the removal of all care related proceedings from the juvenile court under the Children Act 1989 caused confusion as to the exact nature of both care and criminal proceedings (CCLR, 1985; Anderson, 1978). The growth first of the welfare model of juvenile justice, its subsequent fall from favour and the current state of uncertainty as to the ideological basis of juvenile justice in England and Wales has most recently been usefully and comprehensively considered, albeit from a partial 'justice' position, by Morris and Giller (1987). If anything is certain in the juvenile justice system, it is that there is an infinite variety of practice and interpretation of court procedure throughout the whole system from the initial police involvement to the court's sentencing decisions (Anderson, 1978; Ball, 1983; Parker, Casburn and Turnbull, 1981; Priestley, Fears and Fuller, 1977; NACRO, 1984, 1988b; Parker, Sumner and Jarvis, 1989).

Constitution of the youth court

The lay justices who sit in the youth court are elected to the youth court panel for a three-year term by all the magistrates in their petty sessional division, or are selected by the Lord Chancellor for the Inner London panel. They should normally be under the age of 50 when first appointed and have experience of dealing with young people and 'a real appreciation of the surroundings and way of life of the children who are likely to come before the courts' (HO Circular, 1979). The extent to which these requirements are met varies greatly depending on the policies of the individual bench and on the availability of suitable candidates. Youth panel justices are expected to undertake some additional training and are encouraged to visit community homes run by local authorities and prison service establishments for juvenile offenders.

It has been a continuing cause for official concern that, with the substantial reduction in the number of cases coming to court as a result of increased use of cautioning, in some areas the juvenile panels were too large for the amount of work. The result was that individual members were unable to 'obtain sufficient practical experience of this important and specialised work' (HO Circular, 1979). Research showed some evidence of a reduction in the size of panels relative to their sittings, and of an increase in the number of panels made up of a combination of justices from several Petty Sessional Divisions (PSDs) within one clerkship (NACRO, 1988b).

In order to avoid those appearing in the youth court coming into contact with adult offenders, the Rules provide that youth courts should be held, where possible, in a different building or on a different day from adult courts; at the very least, the youth court may not be held in the same room in which an adult court has sat or will sit within one hour (1933 Act, s.47(2)). Arrangements have to be made for separate waiting-areas for those attending youth courts. The physical settings in which they are held and the suitability of the facilities available have been shown to vary as randomly as all other aspects of the juvenile justice system (Hilgendorf, 1981).

Jurisdiction of the youth court

The Children Act 1989 removed care proceedings from the juvenile court, and the Criminal Justice Act 1991 brought 17-year-olds within the jurisdiction of the re-named youth court for trial and sentence, but not for remand purposes (s.68).

Criminal proceedings

There is no criminal responsibility for persons under 10 years of age. Children aged 10–13, and young persons aged 14–17, will have all criminal charges against them heard in the youth court, except where:

1. the charge is one of homicide (1933 Act, s.53(1));
2. a young person is charged with an offence for which the maximum penalty in the case of an adult is 14 years' imprisonment, and the circumstances of the offence are such that a substantial penalty is required, the young person may be committed to the Crown Court for trial (1933 Act, s.53(2));
3. the juvenile is jointly charged with an adult;
4. the juvenile appears in the adult court because of a mistake as to his age.

In the last two circumstances above, the magistrates' court may deal with the case by way of discharge or fine; if it wishes to impose a greater penalty, it must remit the case to the youth court for sentence unless the juvenile is committed to the Crown Court under section 53(2). Use of this section has more than doubled within the past decade, from 65 in 1980 to 177 in 1988. This and other important anomalies about the use of the provision are addressed in the report of a NACRO Working Group (NACRO, 1988a).

Arrest and the criminal process

Juveniles arrested by the police have rights regarding arrest and interrogation under the Police and Criminal Evidence Act 1984, in addition to those for adults described in Chapter 3. For the purposes of detention and remand 17-year-olds are treated as adults and not juveniles.

1. Juveniles may not be arrested or interviewed at school, except in exceptional circumstances (1984 Act, Code C, para. 11.15).

2. When a juvenile is brought to a police station under arrest, the custody officer must contact the 'appropriate adult' (see p. 37) and ask them to attend the police station; questioning of the juvenile must not begin before the adult arrives unless authorized in cases of grave urgency by a superintendent or officer above (s.13.1).
3. Juveniles, like adults, must be informed of their right to have a solicitor present at the police station; if the appropriate adult considers that legal advice should be taken, interrogation must not start until such advice has been obtained.
4. Juveniles should not be detained in police cells unless there is nowhere else they can be properly supervised. They may not be placed in a cell with a detained adult (Code C para. 8.9).
5. The rules relating to the fingerprinting of juveniles are outlined in Chapter 3 (p. 38).

Remand If a juvenile is charged the provisions of the Bail Act 1986 apply and he must normally be released on bail. If he is not released on bail remand must be to local authority accommodation (Children and Young Persons Act 1969 as amended). Boys of 15 and 16 may under transitory provisions under the Criminal Justice Act 1991, which will last until local authorities have sufficient secure accommodation available to enable custodial remand for juveniles to come to an end, still be remanded to prison establishments. Where a court is of the opinion that the criteria in the amended section 23 (5) of the Children and Young Persons Act 1969 apply, and that only remanding him to a remand centre or prison would 'be adequate to protect the public from serious harm from him', it may remand a 15- or 16-year-old to a remand centre or, if that is not available, to prison.

Legal aid is available in the youth court subject to parental means and the same criteria as in the adult court, except that legal representation must be offered when care or custodial sentences are being considered, unless the defendant refuses to apply for legal aid or to consult a solicitor.

Diversion from the criminal process
As with all aspects of the juvenile justice system, the process whereby a juvenile who is arrested or reported by the police

for committing a criminal offence receives a caution or appears before the youth court varies widely depending on the locality (Priestley, Fears and Fuller, 1977; Richardson, 1989). Most police authorities have some form of juvenile liaison scheme or juvenile bureau which operates with the cooperation of the probation, social and education welfare services to divert many offending juveniles, who admit their offences, away from courts by means of a formal police caution. Rates of caution vary widely from one police authority to another but have, on the whole, risen steadily over the past decade (Tutt and Giller, 1983). A Home Office circular issued in 1985 contributed to the increase to 75 per cent in cautioning rates for offenders under 17 by 1989. A more recent circular (1990) sets out national standards to ensure that the same criteria are applied to the cautioning of all offenders, irrespective of age. Its objective is clearly to raise the use of cautioning for adult offenders in line with that achieved for juveniles.

Procedure in court

When a juvenile does appear in court, the procedure followed is a modified version of that for an adult. It is designed to give the defendant the protection of due process, but also to allow parents to have an opportunity to make their views known to the court. Statutorily the youth court is bound to 'have regard to the welfare of the child' when reaching a decision (1933, Act, s.44), yet that duty does not prevent the court from reaching decisions and imposing penalties which may be clearly contrary to the child's interests but which the justices may believe necessary for the protection of the public.

As in summary proceedings in the adult court, the defendant in the youth court is entitled to a summary of the evidence against him if the offence is indictable or one triable either way in the case of an adult (Magistrates' Courts (Advance Information) Rules 1985).

Although many would question whether they achieve their objective, the procedural rules which govern youth court proceedings seek to avoid undue stigma and publicity while maintaining the important principle of open justice. Attendance in court is restricted to those involved in the case and the press, who may publish reports of the proceedings but not any details, such as name, address or school, which might identify the defendant, unless the court rules that it is in the interests of justice that they should be made public. Under revised provisions (1991 Act s.56) a parent or guardian of a child or young person under 16 years is required to attend and stay at court with the juvenile unless the court is satisfied that it would be unreasonable to require attendance. Courts may require the parents of 16- and 17-year-olds to attend if they feel it to be necessary. In a long advocated reform defendants over the age of 15 are now allowed to plead guilty by letter in the same circumstances as defendants in the adult court (Ball, 1981b).

The actual hearing follows only a slightly modified version of adult proceedings, in that the charge must be expressed in simple language and an opportunity given to the parents to express their view as to the propriety of the plea. If there is any doubt whether or not the defendant should admit the offence, the court should err on the side of caution and record a denial. In addition, there is provision for a juvenile to change his plea at any time before the final order is made (*S*. v. *Recorder of Manchester* [1971]).

If the juvenile denies the offence, the trial will follow the normal pattern, with attempts – often not very successful – being made to ensure that an unrepresented juvenile is helped with the cross-examination of prosecution witnesses and other problems of evidence. If the charge is admitted, or after a finding of guilt, the court proceeds to sentence; and at this stage, the court will be made aware of any previous cautions or findings of guilt and will read any reports presented by the local authority.

Reports for the court

Under section 9(1) of the 1969 Act, where children are brought before the court by the local authority in care proceedings or by the police in criminal proceedings:

> It shall be the duty of the authority, unless they are of the opinion that it is not necessary to do so, to make such investigation and provide the court before which the proceedings are heard with such information relating to the home surroundings, school record, health and character of the person in respect of whom the proceedings are brought as appear to the authority likely to assist the court.

This wording gives local authorities considerable discretion as to whether reports should be prepared and as to their content.

Until the mid-1980s it was the practice in all except very minor or motoring cases for social inquiry reports prepared by social services or the probation service, and a report from the offender's school, either to be routinely prepared in advance of the hearing, unless it was known that the charge was being denied, or for the case to be adjourned for reports. During the early eighties considerable research-based disquiet was expressed about the possibility that the content of reports on many juveniles committing minor offences resulted in effectively more severe sentences than was warranted by the offending behaviour (Ball, 1983; Thorpe *et al.*, 1980; Morris *et al.*, 1980; Parker *et al.*, 1989). This evidence combined with policy decisions in the probation service to target their limited resources to providing non-custodial alternatives for serious offenders at risk of custody, and to restrict report-writing to those cases, with the support of social service departments, led to a very marked reduction in the numbers of reports presented to the juvenile court (NACRO, 1988b).

This reduction was achieved, in many areas, by agreement between the juvenile panel and the agencies that reports would not be required for those appearing before the court for the first or possibly second time unless the offence is so serious that the court might be considering a custodial penalty. If in any particular case the court is unwilling to proceed to sentence without the background information which reports would provide, it always has the power under section 9(2) of the 1969 Act to request reports or further information, and unlike the initial provision under subsection 1, the local authority has no discretion; it must comply with the request.

It was apparent in the late 1980s that, in many areas, the reduction of the numbers of social inquiry reports (SIRs) prepared had not been matched by a reduction in school reports, which research evidence showed are often routinely prepared when an SIR would only be available on request after an adjournment (NACRO, 1988b). This gave rise to concern because of evidence of the possible undue influence of educational factors, as brought to the courts' attention through the school court report, on the outcome of criminal proceedings in the juvenile court (Ball, 1981a; Sumner *et al.*, 1988). One of the recommendations in the second NACRO Report on school reports in the juvenile court is that this practice should end and that reports from schools should only be prepared and presented with SIRs, ideally in a single document (NACRO, 1988b).

Many of the larger youth courts have an arrangement with the agencies, much favoured by justices, that in cases in which the bench is reluctant to proceed without any background information, a social worker or probation officer will if the case is adjourned for a short time be available to interview the defendant and his parents and provide the court with a 'stand-down' report as to whether they consider an adjournment for a full report to be necessary.

When reports are presented in youth court proceedings, they are subject to procedural rules which partly as a result of research evidence, and pressure mounted by NACRO (1984), were revised in 1988 to allow parents and defendants access to the contents of all reports with provision to exclude defendants in very limited circumstances. This not only removed a considerable disadvantage suffered by juveniles and their parents as compared with adult defendants who are entitled to see all reports about them presented to the court in criminal proceedings, but also one between the practice regarding SIRs the whole contents of which were generally revealed to parents and defendants, and school reports which were in the majority of courts regarded as confidential to the court (Ball, 1983). Having read any reports and heard any mitigation from a legal representative, or from unrepresented juveniles and parents, the court proceeds to sentence.

Orders in ascending order of severity

The following orders may be made in respect of children found guilty of criminal offences:

(a) *A discharge*, which may be *absolute* or *conditional*, under which if the offender appears in court for a subsequent offence during the period of the condition (max. 3 years), he may be dealt with for the original offence as well as the current one.

(b) *A fine*, subject to a limit of £100 for a child and £400 for a young person. Under section 26 of the Criminal Justice Act 1982, the parent or guardian is required to pay unless he cannot be found or it would be unreasonable to order him to do so having regard to the circumstances of the offence.

Supervision orders
There are five types of supervision order under the 1969 Act, as substantially amended by the Criminal Justice Act 1988, Part IX, and Schedule 10 and further by the 1991 Act; orders may be for a maximum of 3 years:

1. A supervision order, to which may be added the requirements to reside with a particular person who is agreeable (s.12(1)), or a requirement – provided that evidence required under the Mental Health Act 1983 is available – to undergo medical treatment (s.12B).
2. A supervision order with a requirement under section 12(2) to comply with directions given by the supervisor to undertake activities arranged by the supervisor. This provision under section 12(2) is known as 'intermediate treatment', although this term does not appear in the Act.
3. Under section 12A(3), a supervision order with a requirement to undertake activities or to refrain from activities specified by the court.
4. Provided the defendant is of school age and the court, having consulted the local authority, is satisfied that arrangements exist for suitable education, and considers the order necessary to secure good conduct or prevent further offending, an order requiring the juvenile to comply with whatever arrangements for his education are made by his parents and approved by the education authority may be attached to a supervision order (s.12C).
5. In some circumstances, a court making a specified activities requirement under section 12A(3) may, provided the criteria in the Children and Young Persons Act 1969, section 12D, as amended by the 1991 Act, are satisfied, must state in open court why it finds the criteria satisfied and that it is making a supervision order instead of a custodial sentence (s.12D). This has implications if the order is breached (for further details, see Stone (1991a)).

A juvenile who commits a further serious offence whilst on a section 12A(3) supervision order made under section 12A(3) may be brought back to court on an application by the local authority to discharge the supervision and replace it with a requirement for the young offender to live in local authority accommodation for up to six months. Breach of any requirement in a supervision order made in criminal proceedings, except under section 12B, may make a juvenile liable for a fine of up to £100 or an Attendance Centre order. However, if the court has stated that the supervision order with specified requirements (s.12A(3)) was made instead of a custodial sentence, the order may be discharged and the court may order any disposal which could have been imposed for the original offence.

Probation

The 1991 Act (s.8) amends the Powers of the Criminal Courts Act 1973 to allow probation orders to be made on 16-year-olds. The youth court may therefore, subject to the criteria for imposing a community sentence (s.6), choose whether a supervision or probation order is most suitable. Sixteen- and 17-year-olds may also be made the subject of combined community service and probation orders under section 11 or a curfew order (s.12).

Attendance Centre orders   These orders may be made on 10–17-year-old boys and girls where Attendance Centres are available. The order may be for 12–24 hours, except that an offender under age 14 may be ordered less where 12 hours is considered excessive, and should not generally receive more than 12 hours. The order may be for up to 36 hours for 16- and 17-year-olds. The order requires the offender to attend at a centre, to participate in two-hour sessions of physical and craft activities until the hours ordered have been completed.

Proof of breach of an order enables the offender to be dealt with in another way for the original offence. A new Attendance Centre order may be made while an existing one is running, regardless of the numbers of hours still to run.

Care Order   The power to make care orders in criminal proceedings under the 1969 Act section 7(7 and 7A) was abolished by the Children Act 1989 and replaced by the power, referred to above (p.107), to make a requirement of residence in local authority accommodation, provided that the criteria added to the 1969 Act in section 12AA are satisfied.

Community Service order

Under section 68 of the 1982 Act and Schedule 12 as amended, a Community Service order (CSO) may be made on 16- and 17-year-olds subject to a maximum of 240 hours, provided he consents and the court is satisfied that a scheme exists and that the offender is a suitable candidate for such work and can be accommodated within the scheme.

Custodial sentences

Under the Criminal Justice Act 1988 a single sentence of detention in a young offender institution replaced detention centre and youth custody orders for young male offenders aged 14–20 and females of 15–20. Efforts during the passage of the 1991 Bill to raise the age for liability to custody for boys to 15 years succeeded where similar pressures in 1988 failed despite the best endeavours of the concerned agencies and organizations (Children's Society, 1988). The criteria for imposing custodial sentences on young offenders, introduced in the Criminal Justice Act 1982 and amended by the 1988 Act, have been further revised and extended to all offenders of 15 years or more, except those charged with an offence carrying a penalty fixed by law (Wasik and Taylor, 1991). Such sentences may be passed only if the court is satisfied, on grounds which must relate to the offender, that no other method of dealing with the defendant is appropriate because:

a)   the offence, or the combination of the offence and one other associated with it, was so serious that only such a sentence can be justified for the offence; or

b)   where the offence is a violent or sexual offence, that only such a sentence would be adequate to protect the public from serious harm from him.

Where a defendant refuses to give consent to a community sentence a custodial sentence may be passed even if the above criteria are not met (Criminal Justice Act 1991 s.1).

Hospital or Guardianship order under the Mental Health Act 1983

This is very rarely used. Hospital or Guardianship orders under the Mental Health Act 1983, section 37, are very occasionally used where the offence is imprisonable in the case of an adult and the court has medical evidence that the child is suffering from mental illness, psychopathic disorder or severe mental impairment. A Hospital order can only be made if the condition is treatable and Guardianship orders are only available to the youth court for children of age 16 years.

Additional orders
The youth court can impose other orders in addition to disposal.

1. *Compensation*   Under section 67 of the Criminal Justice Act 1982, compensation to the victim for damage or injury may be awarded either in addition to, or instead of, another disposal. If the offender's means are insufficient to pay a fine and compensation, the court must give preference to compensation.
2. Costs.
3. Deprivation of property used for criminal purposes.

Parental responsibility
Financial orders   In line with the thinking outlined in the white paper Crime, Justice and Protecting the Public (Home Office 1990) the duty to require parents or guardians of young offenders to pay any fines or compensation imposed by a criminal court is amended under the 1991 Act in the case of offenders of 16 and 17 years to a power. The duty remains in regard to offenders aged 10–15.

The lengthy and bizarre saga of local authorities liability, or more recently lack of liability (*Leeds City Council* v. *West Yorkshire Metropolitan Police* [1983] 1 AC 29), to pay fines and particularly compensation imposed on juveniles committing offences whilst in care, has been statutorily resolved by section 57 of the 1991 Act which brings local authorities within the definition of parent or guardian under section 55 of the Children and Young Persons Act 1933. For the purposes of unit fines the unit value is the maximum for the offender's age (£5 for under 14 and £20 for 14–17 years). No account has to be taken of means to pay when compensation is awarded (Wasik and Taylor, 1991).

Binding over   The government's original proposals which aimed, by greater use of recognisances, at increasing parental responsibility for their offending children met a barrage of opposition and those finally included in section 58 are not radically different from previous provisions contained in the Children and Young Persons Act 1969. The main difference is the requirement that the court should give its reasons when deciding not to bind over a parent or guardian in the recognisance of a sum of up to £1000 for the young offender's future good behaviour.

Pressure for change

It is generally accepted that custody for juveniles is damaging and, as reconviction rates following any custodial sentence are uniformly high (75–80 per cent), ineffective. Over recent years considerable progress has been achieved by local authority social service departments, and the probation service, working with the police, to reduce the number of juveniles appearing in court. Both the agencies and the voluntary sector have also, encouraged by funding resulting from a DHSS initiative in 1983, provided community-based programmes which have been widely used by courts as an alternative to custodial sentences, and have contributed significantly to the overall reduction of custodial sentences for juveniles from 7,000 in 1981 to fewer than 2000 in 1990. However, geographical comparisons show that there are a number of areas dealing with similar offenders committing similar offences in which custody rates are still very high, and there are concerns that unintended consequences of the changes in jurisdiction and sentencing introduced by the Children Act 1989 and the Criminal Justice Act 1991 could result in a reversal of this trend (Ball, 1992).

Glossary of legal terms

Affidavit	Written statement made for the purposes of proceedings and signed and sworn or affirmed before an authorized official.
Certiorari	Order of the High Court to review and quash the decision of a lower court which was based on an irregular procedure.
Cross-examination	Questions put to a witness by other parties to test out evidence given.
Discovery of documents	Disclosure of documents to other parties before proceedings.
Estoppel	A rule which prevents a person denying the truth of a statement or the existence of facts which that person has led another to believe.
Examination 'in chief'	The interrogation of a witness by those who have called him.
Ex parte	Application made by one party in the absence of other parties (e.g. place of safety orders).
Functus officio	The position of a person who having had authority to act has discharged it and is no longer authorized to act.
Guardian *ad litem*	Guardian for the duration of the legal proceedings.
Hearsay evidence	Evidence of facts in issue which are not within the direct knowledge of the

	witness, but have been communicated to him by another.
Indictment	Written accusation charging a Crown Court defendant.
Injunction	Court order requiring someone to do or refrain from doing something.
Inter partes	Proceedings in which all parties are heard.
Interim	Literally 'in the meantime', an order made before the full hearing.
Lacuna	A gap in the law.
Leading question	Question suggesting the required answer, or one which can only be answered 'yes' or 'no'.
Mandamus	Command from the High Court to a lower court to do what is required.
Mens rea	The guilty intention to commit a crime.
Next friend	The person through whom a minor or mental health patient acts in legal proceedings.
Obiter dictum	Statement of opinion by a judge which is not directly relevant to the case being tried.
Plaintiff	The person who brings a civil action.
Prohibition	Order of the High Court preventing a lower court from exceeding its jurisdiction or acting contrary to the rules of natural justice.
Putative father	The man not married to the child's mother and alleged to be the father.
Ratio decidendi	The reason for a judicial decision.
Re-examination	Questions put to the witness by the person calling him after cross-examination.
Statutory instrument	Subordinate legislation made in exercise of a power granted by statute.
Sub judice	During the course of a legal trial or under consideration.
Subpoena	Court order that a person attends court to give evidence or to produce documents.

Ultra vires   An act outside the authority conferred by law.

Bibliography

Alison, N. (1980), *Rights and Risks*, London: National Corporation for the Care of Old People.

Allen, N. (1990), *Making Sense of the Children Act 1989*, Harlow: Longman.

Anderson, R. (1978), *Representation in the Juvenile Court*, London: Routledge and Kegan Paul.

Ball, C. (1981a), 'The use and significance of school reports in Juvenile Court criminal proceedings: a research note', *British Journal of Social Work*, **11**(4), 479–83.

Ball, C. (1981b), 'Minor motoring offences committed by juveniles: the case for allowing a guilty plea by letter', *Justice of the Peace*, **145**, 10.

Ball, C. (1983), 'Secret justice: the use made of school reports in juvenile courts', *British Journal of Social Work*, **13**(2), 197–206.

Ball, C. (1987), 'Legal representation for the child in adoption proceedings', *Family Law*, **17**, 230.

Ball, C. (1988), 'Legal eye', *Community Care*, 23.9.88, p. 12.

Ball, C. (1989), 'The current and future context of emergency protection', *Adoption and Fostering*, **13**(2), 38–42.

Ball, C. (1990), 'Children Act 1989: Origins, Aims and Current Concerns' in P. Carter, T. Jeffs and M. Smith (eds), *Social Work and Social Welfare Yearbook 2*, Milton Keynes: Open University Press, pp. 1–21.

Ball, C. (1991), *Social Work Law File: Child Care Law*, 3rd edn, Norwich: University of East Anglia.

Ball, C. (1992), 'Young offenders and the youth court', *Criminal Law Review*, April, 277–87.

Ball, C., Harris, R., Roberts, G. and Vernon, S. (1988), *The Law Report: Teaching and Assessment of Law in Social Work Education*, London: CCETSW.

Ball, C., Roberts, G. and Vernon, S. (1991), *Teaching, Learning and Assessing Social Work Law*, London: CCETSW.

Blom-Cooper, L. (1985), *A Child in Trust: The Report of the Panel of Inquiry into the Circumstances Surrounding the Death of Jasmine Beckford*, London Borough of Brent.

Blom-Cooper, L. (1987), *A Child in Mind: The Report of the Commission of Inquiry into the Circumstances Surrounding the Death of Kimberley Carlile*, London: London Borough of Greenwich.

Bottomley, A. K. (1973), *Decisions in the Penal Process*, London: Martin Robertson.

Bottoms, A. (1974), 'On the decriminalisation of the English Juvenile Courts' in R. Hood (ed.), *Crime, Criminology and Public Policy*, London: Heinemann, pp. 319–46.

Braye, S. and Preston-Shool, M. (1990), 'On Teaching and Applying the Law in Social Work: it is not that simple', *British Journal of Social Work*, **20** (4), 333–53.

Bromley, P. M. and Lowe, N. V. (1987), *Family Law*, 7th edn, London: Butterworths.

Burrows, D. (1989), *Civil Legal Aid*, Bristol Law Series.

Butler, Lord (1975), *Report of the Committee on Mentally Abnormal Offenders*, Cmnd 6244, London: HMSO.

Butler-Sloss, Dame Elizabeth (1988), *Report of the Inquiry into Child Abuse in Cleveland*, Cmnd 412, London: HMSO.

CCETSW (1974), *Legal Studies in Social Work Education*, Social Work Curriculum Study Paper 4, London: CCETSW.

CCETSW (1987), *Regulations and Guidance for the Training of Social Workers to be Considered for Approval in England and Wales under the Mental Health Act 1983*, Paper 19.19, London: CCETSW.

CCETSW (1991), *Rules and Requirements for the Diploma in Social Work Training*, Paper 30, 2nd edn, London: CCETSW.

Child Care Law Review (CCLR) (1985), *Child Care Law Review*, London: DHSS.

Clulow, C. and Vincent, C. (1987), *In the Child's Best Interests,* London: Tavistock.

Cooper, J. (1990), *The Legal Rights Manual,* Aldershot: Gower.

Cretney, S. and Masson, J. (1990), *Principles of Family Law*, 5th edn, London: Sweet and Maxwell.

Davies, M. (1985), *The Essential Social Worker*, 2nd edn, Aldershot: Gower.

DoH (1989a), *Introduction to the Children Act 1989,* London: HMSO.

DoH (1989b), *The Care of Children: Principles and Practice in Regulations and Guidance*, London: HMSO.

DoH (1991a), *Children Act 1989 Guidance and Regulations,* London: HMSO:

Vol. 1   Court Orders

Vol. 2   Family Support, Day Care and Educational Provision for Young Children

Vol. 3   Family Placements

Vol. 4   Residential Care

Vol. 5   Independent Schools

Vol. 6   Children with Disabilities

Vol. 7   Guardians ad Litem and other Court Related Issues

Vol. 8   Private Fostering and Miscellaneous

Vol. 9   Adoption Issues

DoH (1991b), *Working Together under the Children Act 1989*, London: HMSO.

DHSS (1976), *A Review of the Mental Heath Act 1959*, London: HMSO.

DHSS (1986), *Secure Accommodation (No. 2) (Amendment) Regulations,* LAC/86/13, London: HMSO.

DHSS (1987), *The Law on Child Care and Family Services,* Cmnd 62, London: HMSO.

DHSS (1988), *Panel Administration: A Guide to the Administration of Panels of Guardians ad Litem and Reporting Officers,* London: DHSS.

DHSS (annual), *A Guide to Non Contributory Benefit for Disabled People*, Leaflet HB5, London: DHSS.

Disability Alliance (annual), *Disability Rights Handbook*, 25 Denmark Street, London WC2H 8NJ.

Dyde, W. (1986), *Place of Safety Orders*, Norwich: University of East Anglia Social Work Monographs No. 52.

Eckelaar, J. and Dingwall, R. (1990), *The Reform of Child Care Law*, London: Routledge.

Freeman, M. D. A. (1987), *Dealing with Domestic Violence*, Bicester: CHH Editions Ltd.

Gostin, L. (1975), *A Human Condition: The Mental Health Act from 1959 to 1975: Observations, Analysis and Proposals for Reform*, London: MIND, Vol. 1.

Gostin, L. (1978), *The Great Debate: MIND's Comments on the White paper; The Review of the Mental Health Act 1959*, London: MIND.

Gostin, L., Meacher, M. and Olsen, M. R. (1983), *The Mental Health Act 1983: a Guide for Social Workers*, Birmingham: BASW.

Griffiths, A., Grimes, R. H. and Roberts, G. (1990), *The Law and Elderly People*, London: Routledge.

Hilgendorf, L. (1981), *Social Workers and Solicitors in Child Care Cases*, London: HMSO.

HMSO (1966), *Legal Aid in Criminal Proceedings* (Widgery Report), Cmnd 2934, London: HMSO.

HMSO (1978), *The Report of the Committee of Enquiry into the Education of Handicapped Children and Young People* (Warnock Report), Cmnd 7212, London: HMSO.

HMSO (1984), *Second Report of the Social Services Committee (1983–4): Children in Care* (Short Report), HC 360–1.

HMSO (1986), *22nd Report of the Criminal Injuries Compensation Board*, Cmnd 42, London: HMSO.

Hoggett, B. (1990), *Mental Health Law*, 3rd edn, London: Sweet and Maxwell.

Hoggett, B. (1987), *Parents and Children: The Law of Parental Responsibility*, 3rd edn, London: Sweet and Maxwell.

Home Office (1979), Home Office Circular 138/79.

Home Office (1985), *Code of Practice for the Identification of Persons by Police Officers*, London: HMSO.

Home Office (1990), *Crime, Justice and Protecting the Public*, Cmnd 965, London: HMSO.

Jackson, S. (1987), *The Education of Children in Care*, Bristol Papers in Applied Social Studies, University of Bristol.

Judicial Statistics (1986), London, HMSO.

Law Commission (1985), *Review of Child Law: Guardianship*, Working Paper No. 91, London: HMSO.

Law Commission (1986), *Illegitimacy*, 2nd Report, Cmnd 9913, London, HMSO.

Law Commission (1987a), *Care, Supervision and Interim Orders in Custody Proceedings,* Working Paper 100, London: HMSO.

Law Commission (1987b), *Wards of Court*, Working Paper No. 101, London: HMSO.

Law Commission (1988), *Family Law Review of Child Law: Guardianship and Custody*, London: HMSO.

Lawson, E. (1991), 'Are Gillick Rights Under Threat?' *Childrights*, October 1991, No. 80, 17–21.

Levenson, H. and Fairweather, F. (1990), *Police Powers*, London: Legal Action Group.

Liell, P. and Saunders, J. B. (1987), *The Law of Education*, 9th edn, London: Butterworths.

Lowe, N. V. and White, R. (1986), *Wards of Court*, 2nd edn, London: Barry Rose.

Lustgarten, L. (1980), *Legal Control of Racial Discrimination*, London: Macmillan.

McDonnell, P. and Aldgate, J. (1984), *Reviews of Children in Care*, Barnett House Papers, Oxford.

Masson, J. and Shaw, M. (1988), 'The work of guardians ad litem', *Journal of Social Welfare Law*, 3, 164–84.

Millham, S., Bullock, R., Hosie, K. and Haak, M. (1986), *Lost in Care: The Problems of Maintaining Links between Children in Care and their Families,* Aldershot: Gower.

Moeran, E. (1982), *Practical Legal Aid,* London: Oyez Longman.

Moore, J. (1992), *The ABC of Child Protection*, Aldershot: Ashgate.

Morris, A. and Giller, H. (1987), *Understanding Juvenile Justice,* London: Croom Helm.

Morris, A., Giller, H., Szwed, E. and Geach, H. (1980), *Justice for Children*, London: Macmillan.

Murch, M. (1980), *Justice and Welfare in Divorce*, London: Sweet and Maxwell.

Murch, M. 1984), *Separate Representation for Parents and Children: An Examination of the Initial Phase,* Family Law Research Unit, University of Bristol.

NACRO (1984), *School Reports in the Juvenile Court,* London: NACRO.

NACRO (1987), *Time for Change: Report of the Juvenile Crime Advisory Committee,* London: NACRO.

NACRO (1988a), *Grave Crimes: Grave Doubts: Reports of the NACRO Working Group on Sentences Made under s.53 of the Children and Young Persons Act 1933,* London: NACRO.

NACRO (1988b), *School Reports: A Second Look,* London: NACRO.

Packman, J., with Randall, J. and Jacques, N. (1986), *Who Needs Care? Social Work Decisions about Children,* Oxford: Basil Blackwell.

Pannick, D. (1985), *Sex Discrimination Law,* Oxford: Clarendon Press.

Parker, H., Casburn, M. and Turnbull, D. (1981), *Receiving Juvenile Justice,* Oxford: Basil Blackwell.

Parker, H., Sumner, M., and Jarvis, G. (1989), *Unmasking the Magistrates,* Milton Keynes: Open University Press.

Priestley, P., Fears, D. and Fuller, R. (1977), *Justice for Juveniles,* London: Routledge and Kegan Paul.

RCCL (1985), *Review of Child Care Law: Report to Ministers of an Interdepartmental Working Party,* London: HMSO.

Rashid, S. O. and Ball, C. (1987), *Social Work Law File: Mental Health, Disability, Homelessness and Race Relations,* Monograph, UEA, Norwich.

Richardson, N. (1989), *Justice by Geography III,* Manchester: Social Information Systems Ltd.

Rowe, J. (1989), 'Caring Concern', *The Guardian,* 2.6.89.

Sinclair, R. (1984), *Decision Making in Statutory Reviews on Children in Care,* Aldershot: Gower.

Stein, M. (1991), *Leaving Care and the 1989 Children Act,* Leeds: First Key.

Stevenson, O. (1988), 'Law and Social Work Education: a commentary on The Law Report', *Issues in Social Work Education,* **8**(1), 37–45.

Stone, K. (1987), *The Statementing Process,* Social Work Monograph No. 51, UEA, Norwich.

Stone, N. (1991a), *Social Work Law File: Probation Law,* 3rd Edition, Monograph, UEA, Norwich.

Stone, N. (1991b), *The Criminal Process,* Monograph, UEA Norwich.

Street, H. and Brazier, R. (1986), *De Smith on Constitutional and Administrative Law*, 5th edn, Harmondsworth: Penguin.

Sumner, M., Jarvis, J. and Parker, H. (188), 'Objective or objectionable: school reports in the Juvenile Court', *Youth and Policy*, **23**, 14–18.

Thoburn, J. (1988), *Child Placement: Principles and Practice*, Aldershot: Gower.

Thoburn, J. (1991), *Review of Research Relating to Adoption*, Inter-Departmental Review of Adoption Law Background paper DoH.

Thorpe, D., Smith, D., Green, C. and Paley, J. (1980), *Out of Care: The Community Support of Juvenile Offenders*, London: Allen and Unwin.

Tinker, A. (1985), *The Elderly in Modern Society*, 2nd edn, London: Longman.

Tutt, N. and Giller, H. (1983), 'Police cautioning of juveniles: the practice of diversity', *Criminal Law Review*, 587–95.

Vernon, J. and Fruin, D. (1986), *In Care, A Study of Social Work Decision Making*, London: National Children's Bureau.

Vernon, S., Harris, R. and Ball, C. (1990), 'Towards Social Work Law: Legally Competent Professional Practice' (Paper 4.2), London: CCETSW.

Walker, N. (1985), *Sentencing: Theory, Law and Practice*, London: Butterworths.

Wasik, M. and Taylor, R. D. (1991), *Criminal Justice Act 1991*, London: Blackstone Press.

Zander, M. (1990), *Police and Criminal Evidence Act 1984*, revised 2nd edn, London: Sweet and Maxwell.

Name index

Subject index